BELIEVE.

BEHAVE.

BECOME.

**What They Never Told You
About Changing Your Life**

Believe. Behave. Become: What They Never Told You About Changing Your Life
Copyright © 2025 by Jeffrey Vickers
All rights reserved.

No part of this publication may be reproduced, distributed, or transmitted in any form or by any means — including photocopying, recording, or other electronic or mechanical methods — without the prior written permission of the author, except in the case of brief quotations embodied in critical reviews and certain other noncommercial uses permitted by copyright law.

For permission requests, contact the publisher:

Jeffrey Vickers
Tuscumbia, Alabama

ISBN: 978-1-7371940-3-3
Cover Design: Jeffrey Vickers
Interior Layout: Jeffrey Vickers

Printed in the United States of America
First Edition

DEDICATION

This is for the version I was when I penned "Sober Slogans." I'm proud of you, Jeff. You stayed the course. Keep seeking His face. Keep your promise...

For the version I was in active use, (years 14-47): I wonder if this version I am today has met you in your dreams, to comfort you. I'm still here, sending love to you. The journey was worth it.

For the innocent version, (years 1-14): I love you, I love you, I love you. Just know that nothing goes unnoticed. Your God, your ancestors, and personal guides will ALWAYS have your back. Forgive the adults who took your innocence, for they knew not what they did. But you? You are one of the chosen, meant to endure hell, for the purpose of helping others find their personal heaven. Believe, child... believe.

It's amazing what's possible when we **believe.**

TABLE OF CONTENTS

DEDICATION V

INTRODUCTION 1

THE STORY YOU TELL IS THE LIFE YOU LIVE 4

YOU DON'T SEE REALITY YOU PREDICT IT — 17

WHOSE BELIEFS ARE YOU LIVING? 32

BELIEF AS ENERGY, NOT JUST THOUGHT 49

FAITH ISN'T BLIND, IT'S CREATIVE 68

YOUR EMOTIONS ARE GUIDANCE SYSTEMS 84

YOUR BODY HEARS EVERYTHING YOUR MIND SAYS 96

BEHAVING LIKE THE FUTURE YOU 118

RECLAIMING PLAY, AND CREATIVITY 130

YOU ARE NOT BROKEN YOU ARE BECOMING 147

YOU ARE THE UNIVERSE REMEMBERING ITSELF 165

WALK LIKE IT'S ALREADY DONE 178

YOU WERE THE BLUEPRINT ALL ALONG 195

RESOURCES - YOUTUBE BREAKS 208

RESOURCES - PUBLIC FIGURES 210

INTRODUCTION

Believe. Behave. Become.
You've been told a lot of things about who you are. Some of them were lies. Some were just stories that weren't true.

If you're reading this book, maybe it's because you're ready to rebuild. Perhaps you're in recovery. Maybe you're rebuilding after jail, heartbreak, trauma, or just years of surviving. Maybe you're tired of pretending you're okay when you're barely holding on.

I want to tell you something right away: ***You are not broken. You are becoming.***

This book isn't here to fix you — because you don't need fixing. It's here to help you remember who you are, rewrite the story you've been living, and learn how to walk like the version of yourself that already lives inside you.

Nobody Taught Us This
Nobody taught us that our thoughts could be challenged.
Nobody told us that our beliefs could be rewritten.
Nobody said that emotions are guidance systems.

What Makes This Book Different
This book isn't about pretending everything is fine.
It's about teaching you how to:

- Face what's really there
- Act like the person you want to be
- And walk like it's already done

Our journey is broken down into three phases. If you believe in the possibility of change, from the inside out, then keep reading, because it gets better.

The Journey Ahead
1. BELIEVE
You'll learn to identify old stories, challenge toxic beliefs, and create new inner scripts that match who you want to become, not who you've been.
2. BEHAVE
You'll learn how to act in alignment with that new identity — in your thoughts, body, routines, emotions, and central nervous system.
3. BECOME
You'll stop chasing healing and start embodying wholeness — fully, freely, and from within.

This is not just a book. It's a blueprint. Not to "fix" you... just to remind you of the power that's always been inside you.

JEFF VICKERS

SECTION ONE

BELIEVE

(CHAPTERS 1-6)

CHAPTER ONE

The Story You Tell is The Life You Live

It's 6:03 a.m. The mirror is fogged. A sentence lands before the coffee does: "Don't get your hopes up." Pause here—who told you that?

Rewrite the Script

Have you ever stopped to ask yourself,
"Where did I get these thoughts about myself?"
Not just the loud ones — like:

**"I mess everything up"
or
"I'll never get it right."**

But also, the quiet ones that shape your whole day:

**"I'm not smart enough."
"I'm just an addict/felon/lost cause."**

Those thoughts didn't fall from the sky.
They were handed to you.
Some by parents. Some by society...

But here's the twist nobody tells you — just because you inherited a story doesn't mean you have to keep it.

We All Have a Story in Our Heads

We're living out a mental script — like a movie that keeps playing inside our heads. We all love a great movie!

This script says:

- Who we think we are
- What we think we deserve
- What we believe is possible

Most of us didn't choose the script. We didn't sit down and write, "I want to feel worthless. I want to keep sabotaging myself." Of course not. That script was written for survival.

For some, the story came from growing up in chaos — parents who were absent, abusive, or broken themselves. For others, it came from labels —

- **"Troublemaker."**
- **"Slow."**
- **"Unfixable."**
- **"Junkie."**

For a lot of us, it came from silence — nobody ever showed us we could be more.

We got handed a script, and we memorized it.

Real-life example?

When Andre got out of prison, he kept hearing, "Don't expect much — just be grateful you're out."

That script told him to shrink his dreams.
But what if his story wasn't just about survival?
What if it was about redemption?

We Are a Storytelling Species

We're the only creatures on Earth who use language to build identity. We don't just tell stories — we become them.

Think about it:
A dog doesn't sit in the corner thinking,
"I'm a bad dog because I chewed the couch."

A cat doesn't get depressed because it failed to catch a mouse.

But humans?

We create entire lives around what we think we "are" — even if that identity came from pain.

- "I'm broken."
- "I'm hard to love."
- "I'm a screw-up."

If nobody teaches you to challenge the script, you'll keep living the same chapter over and over — with new people, same patterns.

This is why healing is hard.
You're not just quitting drugs.
You're quitting a storyline.

Pause and Reflect
What story have you been telling yourself lately?

Be real...
That people always leave?
That you'll never change?
That you're cursed or unlucky?

Now ask yourself this:

But would you say that about someone you love?

Would you look at your little cousin, your child, or your best friend and say: ***"You're just broken forever."***
Of course not. So why say it to yourself?

Journal Prompt
Top 3 beliefs you've been carrying that no longer serve you?

Now cross them out — literally — and write next to each: "This is a story. Not a fact."

Personal Reflection

I've loved stories since I was a child. My first exposure to great adventures came from my grandmother. While she didn't engage with me much, she did believe in learning. She worked for the Board of Education in The Bronx for over two decades.

One of the coolest things she ever did was buy me the *Encyclopedia Britannica* back when they were sold door to door. I poured into those volumes and went on countless adventures and became whoever I wanted to be.

If I read about a land in one volume, I'd become the famous explorer I discovered in another. Every story placed me as the hero. But later, I lost that feeling of empowerment and instead became the victim in my own vignettes.

Applying the skills you'll learn about allowed me to start writing those self-empowerment stories again. And I want to help you do the same. I want to help you be your hero again.

YouTube Break:
"Change Your Story, Change Your Life" – Tony Robbins

In this video, Tony Robbins breaks down how the story we tell ourselves shapes everything.

He says:
***"Divorce the story of your limitations.
Marry the truth of your potential."***

That line right there?
That's your turning point.

Beliefs Are Not Facts

Let's get real. In recovery, we hear a lot about "changing your life" — but nobody gives us the manual on how to change.

Here's the truth:
A belief is just a thought you've had over and over again until your brain locked it in, like a tattoo.

If someone told you at 6 years old, "You're too much," and you kept hearing it, eventually your brain would start whispering: *"Don't speak up. You'll just push people away."*

But guess what?
Beliefs aren't laws of the universe.
They're mental habits.
And habits can be broken.

The Belief Tax (quick calc)
- Old belief: _____
- 3 ways it cost me this month (time/money/opportunity): 1) ____ 2) ____ 3) ____
- Total "tax" paid: _____

Loop Map: Trigger → Thought → Body → Behavior → Result → *Reinforces Thought*
New Route: Trigger → *Name it:* "Story" → New Thought → Tiny Act

9

Let's Try This Together...

Old belief:
"I'll always be an addict."

Question it:
Who told me that?
Is that 100% true?
What's the cost of keeping that belief?

New belief:
"I'm in recovery — I'm healing and growing."

Say it.
Write it.
Feel it in your body.
That's how we begin to shift.

The Science Behind It

Neuroscience refers to this process as *neuroplasticity* — the brain's ability to change itself.

Dr. Joe Dispenza explains it like this:
"Every time you think a thought; your brain sends out signals. Repeat it? The brain builds a stronger connection. Now it's your default."

It's like walking through grass.
Keep walking and the grass becomes a trail.
That's what your brain does with thoughts.
But here's the beauty:
If you **stop** walking that path...
and **start** walking a new one...
your brain will **build a whole new trail.**

YouTube Break
"The Power of Neuroplasticity" – Joe Dispenza

Let this remind you: Your brain is not broken — it's just trained. And training can be changed.

Story in Action: Meet Kayla

Kayla grew up with chaos.
By age 5, she'd watched her mom get high on the couch.
By 10, she was running away.
By 15, she was pregnant and expelled.
By 21, she was in jail for the third time, using anything.

The script in her head:
"I ruin everything."
"I was never meant to be anything."

One day, inside a recovery group, the counselor looked her in the eyes and said:

> "You're not broken. You're following a script that was handed to you — but it's not the only script."

That shattered something...

Later, Kayla wrote:
"That day, I stopped seeing myself as a mistake — and started seeing myself as a miracle in progress."

Today she's three years clean, working with at-risk teens.
She didn't just get sober.
She changed her story.

Rewrite the Script

Nobody tells us this — but I will:
**You don't have to keep living a story that hurts you.
You can decide, right now, to write a new one.**

Try these:
"I used to be lost, but now I'm learning."
"I survived things others couldn't."
"I'm not just recovering — I'm rebuilding."
"I'm not broken — I'm breaking cycles."
"I'm not cursed — I'm chosen to rise."
**This isn't toxic positivity.
This is radical authorship.**

You're not faking a new identity — you're remembering who you were before the world changed your story.

And that remembering is what's going to change the trajectory of your entire family.

But it starts first, with you...
Because someone **MUST** go first.

Someone must be the one who says:
"This pain stops with me."
"This shame doesn't belong to me."
"This is not my final chapter."
**Let that someone be you.
Let today be the turning point.**

"My Old Story vs. My New Story"

Step 1: My Old Story
Write down one old belief you've been carrying:
"I always mess things up," or "I'm just not good enough."

Step 2: Question It
Ask yourself:
Who gave me that belief?
Was it true every time?
What did it cost me to believe this?
What might my life look like if I let it go?

Step 3: Replace It
Create a new version:

1) "I'm learning how to succeed. I've made mistakes, but I grow from them."
2) "My active use was only Part One of my story. This is the sequel, and I am the hero."

Repetition = Rewiring.
Again, repetition = rewiring.
Again...

You Are Not Your Past

This chapter isn't about pretending life didn't hurt.
It's not about "just thinking positive."

It's about reclaiming your mind from the lies that pain and people handed you.

Because the story you tell is the life you live.
And you, my friend, are the author now.
So... what story do you want to write next?

Journal Prompt
Write a one-sentence story that starts with:
"I am becoming..."

Post it somewhere visible.
Say it daily.
Believe it.

Your New Chapter Starts Here

Just remember that you are the hero of this story, and this must be seen in every chapter.

Truth be told, you are the writer, protagonist, antagonist, and supporting characters in this story — your story.

If you commit to writing daily, one day you will learn this. **So, pick up the pen with purpose.**

You've carried enough pain—now it's time to take power. Each word you write with your actions, thoughts, and beliefs becomes the ink of transformation.

Repetition = Rewiring.
Again, repetition = rewiring.
Again...

Identity Reframe:
Who Am I Becoming?

Part 1: The Old Story
Write down the beliefs or labels you've carried that no longer

serve you. These may have been given to you by others or shaped by painful experiences.

Examples:
"I'm just a screw-up."
"I'll always be an addict."
"I ruin everything I touch."

Part 2: Where Did That Come From?
Trace those old stories back. Who gave them to you? What experience first planted them?

Example:
"I heard my mom say I'd never amount to anything."

Part 3: Is It Still True?
Now ask yourself: Is this belief true today? Has anything changed?

Example:
"I used to believe I was broken. But now I know I was just surviving."

Part 4: The New Identity
Write 2–3 bold, present-tense statements about who you are becoming. These should not be rooted in your past mistakes or pain, but in your current growth, your highest vision for yourself. Speak as the version of you who has already stepped into this new identity.

Examples:
"I am a whole person who chooses healing daily."
"I am a creator, not a victim."
"I am learning to love myself out loud."

Bonus Prompt: Future You Speaks

Imagine your future self — 1 year from now — has stepped into their full power.

What do they say to you today?
"Hey [Your Name], I want you to know…"

Write it out:

_____
_____
_____

Every word you just wrote is more than imagination — it's a seed. Each time you revisit those words, you water that seed with belief. Your future self is not a stranger; they are you, already becoming, yet waiting for you to meet them.

Carry their voice with you as you move forward, and let it guide your choices, your mindset, and your next chapter.

CHAPTER TWO

You Don't See Reality You Predict It —

BELIEVE. BEHAVE. BECOME.

"Your Brain Is Not a Mirror — It's a Projector."
— *Dr. Lisa Feldman Barrett, neuroscientist*

Let's start with a wild truth most people have never heard: **You don't experience the world the way it is.**

You experience the world the way your brain expects it to be. Most of us were never taught this. We assume we're seeing the truth — the facts — as it really is. But that's not what's happening. Your brain doesn't just sit back and wait to react.

It predicts what's going to happen — based on what it already believes. And this is based on past experiences!

Memories!!! Then it fills in the blanks to match that belief. This is why two people can go through the same experience — and walk away with two totally different stories:

- One sees rejection.
- The other sees redirection.
- One sees failure.
- The other sees feedback.

It's not the world that's different — it's the lens they're looking through. Two people can stand in the same place, at the same moment, and yet see completely different realities. One sees obstacles, the other sees opportunities. One focuses on what's missing; the other notices what's possible.

Your reality is shaped by the lens you choose. Adjust your focus, and you'll see growth opportunities that were there all along. Seeing is believing, but what are you choosing to see?

JEFF VICKERS
Real Talk: Why This Matters in Recovery

In recovery, the way we see the world can either lift us into creation mode or pull us back into survival mode.

When you've lived through trauma, addiction, betrayal, or incarceration, your brain learns how to stay ready — for pain, loss, and disappointment. Those patterns were helpful once. They protected you.

But now? Those same predictions can block your healing. If people used to hurt you, your brain might now predict: *"People can't be trusted."*

If you were told "you'll always mess up," your brain might expect: *"I'll relapse eventually — so why even try?"*

If every job turned you down, your brain might whisper: *"They're judging you — don't get your hopes up."*

These aren't just random thoughts. They're predictions — silent assumptions your brain makes based on past pain, not present truth.

And the real danger is this: the more you believe them, the more you unconsciously search for proof that they're right. You filter every moment through that lens.
But that's not recovery.

That's reliving the past in a loop and calling it reality. Recovery means breaking the cycle — choosing to believe something new, even when your mind resists.

BELIEVE. BEHAVE. BECOME.
Your Brain Is a Pattern Machine

Imagine this:
Your brain is like a DJ at a party.
But instead of asking what to play, it keeps spinning the same tracks from your past.

Why?
Because it assumes that's what you expect.

If the world once taught you to expect chaos, disrespect, or failure, your brain keeps playing that playlist — even when the party has changed.

This is why it can be hard to:
- *Feel joy*
- *Accept love*
- *Believe you're safe now*

But guess what?
You don't have to keep vibing to that old track.
You can teach your brain some new music.

Music of **hope.**
Of **growth.**
Of **trust.**

You're not just learning to cope — you're learning to reprogram the DJ.

The Science Behind It

Neuroscientist Dr. Lisa Feldman Barrett explains that 80 to 90 percent of what we "see" isn't even coming from our eyes.

It's coming from the inside — from our brain's predictions.

We don't just see with our eyes.
We see with our expectations.
Your brain is like a prediction machine — guessing what's going to happen based on all your past experiences.

Then it reacts as if those guesses are facts.

Here's an example:
You walk into a room and someone frowns.

Your brain instantly goes:
"They don't like me."

But maybe they just have a headache.
Maybe they're lost in their own world.
Your brain guessed wrong — but you still felt the pain.

YouTube Break:

"Your Brain Predicts Reality" – Lisa F. Barrett

In it, she explains how the brain makes "best guesses" based on past data. You don't see what's real — you see what's familiar to you.

This process is called *predictive coding*. It's fast, automatic, and often unconscious. Learn to pause, since we can interrupt it.

What This Looks Like in Real Life
Say you've been rejected over and over.
People bailed when you needed them.

You were judged, ghosted, betrayed.

BELIEVE. BEHAVE. BECOME.

Now you're in recovery.
You're trying to build new relationships.

But your brain — still trying to protect you — keeps whispering: *"Don't get close. They'll leave too."*

You might:
- Avoid texting back.
- Sabotage good connections.
- Push people away "just in case."

Not because **they're bad.**
Not because **you're bad.**

But because your brain is trying to predict pain before it happens. This is called *anticipatory defense.*

It's not **weakness.**
It's **survival.**

But if you never update the prediction, you'll never give the future a chance to be different.

Think of your brain like a thermostat — not a thermometer...

A *thermometer* just measures what is.
A *thermostat* tries to control what's coming.

If you expect heat, you'll turn the air up.
If you expect cold, you'll brace for it.

Now translate that to your emotions:
- If you expect betrayal, your defenses go up.
- If you expect failure, you don't even try.
- If you expect relapse, the back door is open.

This is how old stories keep repeating.
But in recovery? We get to reset the thermostat.

You get to ask: *"What do I actually want to feel today?"*
And then set your mindset to match.

Interrupting the Prediction

Your brain is a storyteller — and it doesn't always tell the truth. Sometimes, it plays old tapes from pain or trauma, trying to protect you by predicting the worst.

But you are not those thoughts. You are the awareness behind them. And you have the power to choose a different path.

Next time your brain says:
- "This won't work."
- "They're going to leave."
- "You're not good enough."

Try this:

Catch it. "That's a prediction, not a prophecy."
Ask yourself: "What else might be true right now?"
Reframe it: "If I believed I was safe/what would I do next?"

This moment of pause gives you power. It opens a crack in the loop — and that's where healing sneaks in.

Journal Prompt:
Write 3 recent predictions your brain made that weren't 100% true. Now write a more hopeful possibility.

YouTube Break:
"How to Rewire Your Brain" – Dr. Andrew Huberman

In this clip, Dr. Huberman explains how your brain literally rewires itself based on the thoughts you repeat.

He says:
> *"You can't stop a negative thought from showing up, but you don't have to invite it to stay."*

He also teaches simple tools to interrupt fear and negative patterns. These practices help rewire the nervous system.

Story in Action: Meet Rico

Rico got out after 7 years behind bars.
He was focused. Motivated.
He went to meetings, got a sponsor, and applied for work.

But every time someone didn't call back, his brain said:
"You're still a felon. Nobody wants you."

It wasn't just disappointing — it felt personal. Like proof he didn't belong in the "real world."

One night, his sponsor said something that flipped a switch:

> *"Maybe it's not the world rejecting you. Maybe it's your own voice, still echoing in your head."*

That hit hard — because it was true.

Rico realized he didn't need the world to tear him down. He was doing it all on his own — quietly, constantly, and automatically. So, he got curious...

Rico started tracking his thoughts. He noticed how fast his brain jumped to old conclusions.

So, he made a list of replacements — and said them daily:
- "I belong at the table."
- "I'm not my past."
- "Something good is coming."
- "I'm showing up, and that's success today."

It wasn't magic. But slowly, things changed.

He landed a job.
Made a few real friends.
Started seeing himself with new eyes.

Not because the world changed overnight — but because he stopped predicting the worst. And when the old thoughts came back — because they always try — he met them with truth. Doing so opened doors Rico never knew existed.

Day by day, Rico built a new normal.
Not perfect. Not easy.
But **rooted in possibility,** not fear.

Rooted in the belief that maybe, just maybe... he wasn't the problem. He was the pattern-breaker.

Story in Action: Meet Lena

Lena had been sober for 14 months but still avoided dating. Every time someone showed interest, she backed away. Her brain told her, "They'll get bored and leave."

In therapy, she learned to spot the exact moment her "prediction voice" kicked in.

One day, a new friend asked her to dinner.
Her brain: "Don't bother."

Her reframe: "What if this turns into a safe, fun night?"

She said yes.
They laughed until closing time.

It didn't lead to romance — but it cracked open a door she thought was sealed shut.

Science Break: Neuroplasticity

Neuroplasticity is your brain's superpower — its ability to literally rewire itself based on repeated thoughts, feelings, and actions.

Old prediction: "I'm not worth showing up for."
New repetition: "I am worth showing up for."

With enough practice, the old neural path weakens, and the new one becomes your brain's default road.

Guided Visualization: Reset the Mental Thermostat

Close your eyes. Picture a thermostat in your mind — this one controls your emotional temperature. Right now, notice where it's set: Fear? Distrust? Self-doubt? Now, see your hand on the dial. Slowly turn it toward *Trust*. Toward *Possibility*. Toward *Hope*. Lock it in. Feel your body shift as your environment matches the new setting.

Quick Practice: The 3-Minute Prediction Reset

- **Notice** — Write one negative prediction in your phone notes.
- **Name** — Say out loud: "That's my past speaking, not my truth."
- **New Path** — Replace it with a positive possibility and repeat it 3 times.

Predict → Pause → Possibility

Step 1: Predict
Write down a negative thought you often have.
Example: "I always mess up interviews."

Step 2: Pause
Ask yourself:

- Is this a fact or a past-based guess?
- Is this happening now, or am I expecting it?

Step 3: Possibility
Create a new possibility:

- "What if I get this job and they're lucky to have me?"
- "What if I feel calm and confident this time?"
- "What if today is different?"

Say it.
Feel it.
Practice it.
Every time you change the prediction — you create a new outcome.

BELIEVE. BEHAVE. BECOME.

You Are Not Stuck

Your past trained your brain to expect pain, failure and struggle. But your future? It's still unwritten.

You have the power to teach your brain something new.
You have the right to expect joy.
To expect healing.
To expect connection.

And the more you practice those expectations — the more they'll become your new reality.

What's one positive prediction you can make about tomorrow? Write it. Believe it. And step into it — one moment at a time.

Because the future isn't written in stone.
It's shaped by the story you choose to believe today.

Let that story be:
One of **strength.**
One of **healing.**
One of **becoming.**

Even if it's just one small step forward — that step counts. That step rewires something. That step makes you a little more free, and ultimately that's the goal – personal freedom.

So, write the prediction.
Say it out loud.
Then walk like it's already true.

Personal Reflection

When I was in third grade, both my mother and stepdad abandoned me within a two-week period. I was forced to move in with my grandmother and her husband, who were older and didn't engage with me. My grandmother's favorite saying was, *"Children are to be seen and not heard."*

I built an identity out of those experiences — even creating mini-identities. My personal beliefs were shaped daily by the negative messages my brain developed. Being abandoned and then ignored by my caregivers at such a young age damaged my self-worth and influenced every relationship.

Forty years later, I'm still correcting my self-talk, still rewiring my brain, still becoming a new personality. The training is still necessary, but now it's enjoyable. And it can become enjoyable for you, too. Focus on planting the seeds.

One day you'll see the fruit, and then you'll plant a new harvest with better skills — until the garden outside begins to reflect the one within.

Prediction Loop Breaker

What's a Prediction Loop?
A prediction loop is when your brain expects the worst — and your behavior makes it come true.

Step 1: Identify the Loop
Think of a moment when things went wrong in your recovery or relationships. Be honest — even if it was a small situation.

What happened? Write a quick summary.
What did you expect to happen (before it even started)?

- "They're not going to listen."
- "I'm going to mess it up again."
- "Nobody ever shows up for me."

What did you do or say next that matched that prediction?

What did the outcome prove to your brain?
- "See? I was right. People don't care."
- "Told you I'd fail." _____

Step 2: Break the Loop
Now ask: What other outcome could have happened if your belief were different?

Imagine a better version:
What belief would you need to replace the old prediction?
- "People want to support me."
- "I can pause and choose differently."

What small action could match that new belief?
Make it simple, real, and doable. _____

Step 3: Create a New Loop on Purpose
Next time this loop starts to replay... what will you do?

- Pause
- Name the old belief
- Replace it with your new belief
- Choose a different action
- Reflect on the outcome

Write your plan in one sentence:

"Next time I feel _____, I will remind myself _____ and choose to _____."

BONUS JOURNAL PROMPTS
- What's one loop I've been unknowingly repeating?
- Who or what helps me interrupt my old patterns?
- What does my healed self predict about the future?
- How does that feel different in my body?

You don't break loops by force. You don't bully yourself into change or shame yourself into doing better. That only feeds the very cycle you're trying to end.

You break them with *awareness* — by catching the moment your old pattern starts to run. You break them with *belief* — by daring to trust that a different outcome is possible. And you break them with *practice* — by showing up, over and over, until the new response becomes second nature.

Every time you do this, your brain rewires. New neural pathways form. Your body learns a different rhythm. Your mind begins to expect something better.

That's recovery in action. It's not just about avoiding the old pain — it's about building something new in its place. Every time you choose a new response, you're doing more than breaking a habit; you're shifting the trajectory of your story.

You're not just healing — you're *creating*. You're designing a life that feels safe, aligned, and true. And every small choice you make in that direction sends a message to your future: **This is who I am now.**

CHAPTER THREE

Whose Beliefs
Are You Living?

Let's get honest for a moment...

You're standing in front of the mirror.
The light above you flickers, and for a moment, you really see yourself — the weight in your eyes is heavy with trauma.

And then it happens.
That voice in your head starts talking...
"You're too much."
"You're not enough."
"You'll mess this up just like last time."

You can't even remember the first time you heard it. Maybe it was years ago. Perhaps it was from someone you thought loved you. But here it is again — as familiar as your own reflection.

Ask yourself:
1. How much of what you believe about yourself was handed to you — without your permission?
2. Which of your thoughts about your worth or potential are actually someone else's voice in disguise?
3. If you could erase every belief that wasn't truly yours, who would you be then?

Think back to:
The *parent* who said you were "too sensitive."
The *coach* who yelled, "You'll never be anything."
The *street* that taught you to stay cold, stay hard.
The *system* that labeled you: addict, felon, failure.

These beliefs didn't come from your soul. They were planted. Often early. Often by people who were hurting too. And without even realizing it, you might still be living by their script — even though you never agreed to it.

BELIEVE. BEHAVE. BECOME.
The Inheritance Nobody Talks About

We talk a lot about what people inherit —Money. Land. Eye color. Businesses. Last names.

But what about the invisible inheritance?

What about the stuff you never asked for, but got anyway:
- **Beliefs:** "I'm not enough" — the thought that whispers before a job interview.
- **Habits:** Saying "sorry" every time you take up space.
- **Fears:** That tight chest when someone raises their voice, even if they're not mad at you.
- **Wounds:** The ache of remembering the day someone you loved chose the bottle, or the streets over you.
- **Survival patterns:** Shutting down your feelings because that's what kept you safe.

This invisible inheritance doesn't show up in a bank account. It shows up in how you talk to yourself. How you love or don't love yourself. How you show up — or shrink back.

And it often comes from:
1. Parents and grandparents
2. Teachers and neighbors
3. The streets
4. Religion or culture

Here's the truth most people never say out loud:
- Not everything you inherited is yours to keep.
- You can accept the love — and leave the lies.
- You can keep the strength and leave the shame.
- You can keep the lessons and leave the limits.

Belief Tree: Write the belief. Draw three roots: *Who modeled it? When did it "work"? What did it cost?* Then add one new root: *My belief now →* _____.

Real Talk:
If you were raised around chaos, your nervous system might believe chaos is normal.

If love in your house always came with pain, you might push away good love — or not trust it when it comes.

If the people you grew up with always gave up, you might think success is for other people — not you.

And if people constantly told you to "be tough," you might believe that showing emotions makes you weak.

But none of that is the real you…

That's programming.
And programming can be rewritten.

YouTube Break:
"Breaking Generation Trauma" – Dr. Thema Bryant

Dr. Thema — a trauma psychologist and minister — breaks it down. She explains how trauma and limiting beliefs are passed down like family recipes. Just because something was passed down, you don't have to keep cooking it.

I don't know about you, but that's an analogy I can easily remember. My grandmother was an amazing cook, but there are some recipes I wouldn't dare try.

Dr. Thema says:
> ***"Just because it runs in the family doesn't mean it has to run through you."***

That line?
Let it tattoo your soul.

Story in Action: Meet Marcus

Marcus grew up in a house where real men "don't cry" and "handle business with fists."

His dad drank. His mom prayed.
No one talked. Feelings were either ignored or punished.

By 13, Marcus believed:
- "Vulnerability is weakness."
- "Anger is power."22
- "You gotta hurt first before they hurt you."

Fast forward:
He's 29. In recovery. Sitting in a group circle for the first time — sweating, silent, arms crossed.

He's trying to learn how to:
- Talk without yelling
- Feel without numbing
- Connect without fear

But everything in his body says,
> *"This is dangerous."*

Not because it is — but because healing is unfamiliar. And unfamiliar feels unsafe when all you've known is survival.

The problem wasn't that Marcus was bad.
It's that he was programmed to survive, not to feel.

Today, Marcus is learning a new language — one of honesty, softness, and inner strength. Not overnight. But one breath, one group share, one "I'm not okay," at a time.

Where Do Beliefs Come From?

Most of your beliefs didn't come from "logic." (This is the point where most of you nodded in agreement.)

They came from:
Repetition – what you heard over and over again
Emotion – what hurt, scared, or overwhelmed you
Authority – who said it (parent, preacher, cop, teacher)
Environment – what you had to do to survive
Meaning – the story you told yourself

Your brain is like soil. Whatever gets planted — especially in childhood or trauma — tends to grow roots. And the more emotion behind it, the deeper those roots go.

Belief Formation Timeline

While we all have different experiences, there is a process by which beliefs are usually formed:

- **Childhood Experience** → A parent yells "You'll never get it right."
- **Emotional Reaction** → Shame, fear, or confusion flood your nervous system.
- **Belief Formed** → "I'm not good enough."
- **Behavior Pattern** → You stop trying, or overwork to prove yourself.

- **Life Results** → Missed opportunities, toxic relationships, self-sabotage.

Brain Fact: How Beliefs Rewire

When you challenge a belief and replace it with a new thought repeatedly, you're literally changing your brain.

Old neural pathways weaken (like a trail no one walks anymore) while new ones strengthen (like a fresh path cleared through the woods). This is called *neuroplasticity*.

Every "nope, that's not my belief anymore" moment is not just symbolic — it's biological. Research indicates that the brain forms beliefs by associating thoughts with emotional experiences.

That's why one harsh sentence from a parent can echo for decades. But here's the part most of us were never taught:

- You can pull up the weeds.
- You can dig up old roots.
- You can plant something new.

How to Spot a Borrowed Belief

We're already learning not every belief is our own, but how do we know the difference? How can we spot which is which?

Ask yourself:
- Does this belief help me grow?
- Does this belief bring peace or shame?
- Did I choose this — or was it handed to me?

If it keeps you **stuck...**
If it makes you feel **small...**
If it causes you to **self-sabotage...**
It's **not yours** to keep.

Here are some borrowed beliefs people in recovery often carry:
- "I'll always be broken."
- "I don't deserve love."
- "People like me don't change."
- "I'm too far gone."

You didn't come up with those.
They were downloaded into you.
You get to delete them.

Your Inner Voice Might Be Someone Else's

Ever hear that critical voice inside your head?

"You're lazy."
"You'll never get it right."
"You're not worth it."

Now pause...
Whose voice does that really sound like?
- Maybe a parent who never healed.
- Maybe a coach who bullied.
- Maybe society's voice — loud with shame.

The voice in your head might sound like you... but it's not.
The good news? That voice is not permanent.
You can teach your inner voice a new script.

YouTube Break:
"The Lies We Inherit" – Oprah and Dr. Shefali

In this eye-opening conversation, Oprah and Dr. Shefali talk about the false beliefs we absorb from wounded caregivers, culture, and systems we live under.

Dr. Shefali says:
> *"The most radical act of healing is to ask, 'Is this even mine?'"*

Try asking yourself that today.

Personal Reflection

One gift of my recovery is a healthier perspective toward law enforcement. I grew up in The Bronx in the 1980s, when rap music served as commentary on inner-city relationships with policing and systemic injustice.

A few of my favorites from that era were:
1. **"The Message"** – Grandmaster Flash and the Furious Five (1982)
2. **"Dope Man"** – N.W.A. (1987)
3. **"9mm Goes Bang"** – Boogie Down Productions (1987)
4. **"Colors"** – Ice-T (1988)
5. **"F* tha Police"** – N.W.A. (1988)

By 1987, I was conditioned to not trust the police — regardless of race. That belief extended into politics, too. It was a mindset I picked up from both family and the streets, and it reinforced my victim mentality for years.

My recovery journey eventually brought me into relationships with law enforcement and civic partners. I had to look back and understand where my beliefs about government and policing came from, then make the decision to confront them. I realized those beliefs didn't serve me; they only kept me locked in an older version of myself.

Today, I see the value of law enforcement and deeply appreciate their role. I've launched a local reentry initiative, and strong partnerships with law enforcement are critical to our mission's success.

If I hadn't challenged those old beliefs, I'd still be stuck just *thinking* about how to help returning citizens — instead of actively executing a plan.

Healing Starts with Permission

You have permission to:
- Let go of beliefs that were never true
- Redefine what it means to be strong
- Question everything that keeps you stuck

You have permission to say:
1. "They meant well, but they were wrong."
2. "That belief consoled me, but I've grown."
3. "I don't owe loyalty to a story that hurts me."

And with this permission.....
You are not betraying anyone by healing.
You are not being disrespectful by growing.
You are not being fake by breaking cycles.

BELIEVE. BEHAVE. BECOME.
"Who Said That?"

Step 1: List 3 negative beliefs you carry.
Example:
"I always mess things up."
"People leave when they get close."
"I'm not smart enough to succeed."

Step 2: Ask yourself who said it first.
Was it:
- A parent yelling when overwhelmed?
- A partner who projected their pain?
- A teacher who misunderstood you?
- A system that sees your record, not your humanity?

Even if the belief started as your own thought, it may have been shaped by survival — not truth.

Step 3: Rewrite it.
"I'm not a mess-up — I'm a work in progress."
"I'm learning to trust and be trusted."
"I have everything I need to grow."

Say it out loud.
Write it down.
Repeat it daily.

Remember:
The voice in your head can be retrained.

Future Self Rehearsal
Your brain doesn't know the difference between a real experience and one you deeply imagine. This means you can rehearse a better version of yourself — starting now.

Every choice you make trains your brain. Let's give it a preview of the person you're becoming.

STEP 1: MEET YOUR FUTURE SELF
Imagine the version of you who is...
- a) Calm under pressure
- b) Focused in recovery
- c) Kind to themselves
- d) Walking in purpose
- e) At peace with their past

Now answer:
What is this version of you doing each day?
How do they handle challenges differently?
What do they believe about themselves?

STEP 2: DAILY REHEARSAL
Now bring it into the real world.

Pick one area of your life to rehearse today:
- Relationships
- Recovery
- Communication
- Confidence
- Emotions
- Goals

Write one thing your future self would do differently in that area:

> "Instead of yelling, I pause."
> "Instead of isolating, I reach out."
> "Instead of quitting, I ask for help."

Your rehearsal plan:
Now do it. Even if it feels weird.
Even if it's small.
Even if no one notices.
You're not performing — you're practicing.

STEP 2.5: ANCHOR YOUR ENVIRONMENT
Don't rely on memory alone — set reminders around you:
- Sticky note a mirror with your future-self mantra.
- Set an alarm on your phone that pops up mid-day: *"Breathe like your future self."*
- Choose an anchor object — a bracelet, ring, or stone. Each time you touch it, reset into your future self's posture, breath, or thought.

When your environment cues you, practice happens naturally — not just once a day, but all day long. And when you practice all day long, reality responds.

Here's how I do it:
- I play affirmations softly in the background.
- Sometimes I keep one earbud at home.
- Even if I'm just washing dishes or driving, my brain is still running the same program: **belief.**

The point? You don't have to wait for a "perfect moment" to reprogram your mind. Your environment can become "the meditation." This keeps your vibration consistent.

Over time, this repeated input rewires your brain. What started as a chosen practice — affirmations, self-belief, possibility — becomes your default setting, *no matter where you are.* This takes care of "imposter syndrome" for many.

By anchoring your environment, you're feeding your brain fresh data. And your brain will always build from the data you give it.

Think of your brain like a construction site:
- Every thought, word, or sound is a brick.
- Your environment is the supply line delivering those bricks, in real-time.
- Over time, your mind builds structures (beliefs, habits, behaviors) out of whatever material it's given.

If your environment is full of negative cues — constant chaos, toxic conversations, or reminders of your past — your brain has no choice but to build with that material. You'll end up reinforcing the same old structures.

But when you start anchoring your environment with intentional cues — affirmations, supportive people, music that lifts you, reminders of your goals — suddenly, you're delivering new bricks to the site. Your brain now has fresh material to build something different.

The principle is simple: garbage in, garbage out... but also, gold in, gold out.

STEP 3: REFLECT AND RESET
At the end of the day, ask yourself:

Did I show up as my future self?
- Yes
- Kinda
- Not yet

What worked well?
What was hard?
What will I try tomorrow?

BONUS TOOL: "In Character"
When you feel triggered or stuck, pause and ask:
"What would my future-self do right now?"

Then write it like a script.

"*Scene:* I'm feeling overwhelmed. My future-self breathes deeply and says _____."

Use this during journaling or morning rehearsal. Let your nervous system feel the shift. Picture the version of you who already lives the life you're creating. Feel the joy of that version of yourself.

What do they feel in their body?
What do they believe when they wake up?
What do they no longer fear?

Let the music guide you there.
Not just in thought — but in frequency.
This isn't daydreaming.
This is rehearsal for your future. Press play.
Then act as if you already are.

Every time you show up as your future self, you build the bridge from who you were to who you're becoming.

It might feel invisible.
You're not clocking in. No one's clapping.

But your **brain** is rewiring.
Your **nervous system** is adapting.
Your **energy** is aligning.

This is not pretending — it's preparing.

Each time you walk, speak, or breathe like the version of you that already made it... you collapse the distance between now and next. Don't underestimate these moments.

They're **not fantasy. They're blueprints.** And with every **repetition,** you're making the impossible... **inevitable.**
Rehearse. Reinforce. Become.

Closing Truth

You're not just in recovery from drugs or alcohol.

You're in recovery from many things. Time will reveal them, as you continue to work on yourself. These are the areas many of us unknowingly try to deal with during our substance use journey:

- Trauma
- Shame
- Silence
- Unquestioned beliefs

This is deep work. This is real healing. You are not weak for needing to unlearn. You are wise for recognizing it.

Belief by belief, you are taking your life back.
And with every old thought you release,
You make room for a new truth to grow.
You are not your programming.
You are your potential.

Micro-Success Story: 30 Days of Future Self

Janelle, 34, tried "Future Self Rehearsal" for just one month. She set a sticky note on her bathroom mirror that said, "I handle challenges calmly." Each morning, she rehearsed her future self for 2 minutes.

At first, it felt silly. By week 3, she caught herself pausing instead of snapping at her kids. By week 4, her coworkers noticed she was **"calmer under stress."**

Her takeaway?
"I thought I had to become someone brand new. I just had to rehearse who I already was becoming."

This is how belief becomes behavior. It's not about flipping a switch overnight — it's about practicing small rehearsals that rewire your brain and reshape your story.

Your challenge:
Choose one belief you've carried from someone else and rehearse your future self with it for the next 7 days.

When you notice the old voice show up, pause and ask:
- "Whose voice is this, really?"
- "What's my future self rehearsing, instead?"

Every time you answer, you're not just healing the past. You're creating your future.

CHAPTER FOUR

Belief As Energy, Not Just Thought

Let's go deeper...

In Chapters 1–3, we covered how beliefs shape your identity, how many of those beliefs are inherited, and how your brain predicts your life based on your past.

But here's a truth that goes even deeper — a truth that can completely change the way you move through the world:

> Beliefs don't just live in your head.
> They live in your energy.
> **You don't just think beliefs, you feel them.**
>
> You broadcast them — like a signal. And that signal?
> <u>**It's shaping your reality, even if you don't see it.**</u>

More Than Just Thoughts

If beliefs were only thoughts, we could all just say:
1. "I'm strong."
2. "I'm confident."
3. "I love myself."

And **BOOM** — instant healing, right?

But let's be real. You've probably tried that. You've probably tried to "wish" it into existence, and wondered why you're still the same person, day in and day out.

You've told yourself:
A. "I'm worthy."
B. "I'm going to be okay."
C. "I'm going to change my life."

But deep down... something still felt off.

The words felt shaky.
You didn't believe them all the way.

Why?
Because belief isn't just **mental.**
It's **emotional.**
It's **energetic.**

It lives in your body, in your nervous system, and in your vibration. Your body becomes the proof of what you truly believe. The way your chest opens or tightens, the way your breath flows or gets stuck — these are the signals that reveal whether the belief has landed deeper than your thoughts.

You can say the words... But if your energy is still stuck in fear, doubt, or shame — the words won't land. It's not just about what you say. *It's about what you believe beneath the surface.* Your nervous system and the universe know the truth...

Affirmations aren't magic spells — they're tuning forks. If your frequency is off, the words will feel hollow.

But when you align your energy with the truth — that's when the shift begins. So don't just speak it. You must:
- Feel it.
- Live it.
- Become it.

Because when your energy matches your words — the world responds, so please speak wisely. Many ancient texts reveal the power of affirming who we are and what we desire.

Think of it like trying to play a beautiful song on a guitar that's completely out of tune. You can strum the right chords, sing the right lyrics, even close your eyes and feel the moment — but if the strings are tight in the wrong places, the sound will always come out sour. That's what happens when you say the words, but your energy hasn't caught up.

Your nervous system — like those guitar strings — holds tension, fear, and doubt. And no matter how perfectly you repeat your affirmations, the "sound" you're broadcasting into the world is still off.

But the good news? Just like an instrument can be tuned, so can you. The work isn't about forcing louder words — it's about aligning your energy until the note rings true.

You Are Energy First

Everything in this universe is made of energy — including you. This isn't just spiritual talk. It's backed by science.

According to quantum physics, what looks *solid* is really a buzzing field of vibrating particles.

- Your thoughts carry an electrical charge.
- Your emotions have a measurable frequency.
- Your body is 99.999999% empty space.

What fills that space? **Energy.**
And energy is always vibrating — sending out a signal.

How Energy Feels in the Body

- When you feel fear, your body contracts.

- When you feel joy, your body expands.
- Your frequency shifts with every emotion.

That means your **beliefs — if truly felt — shape the energy you move with.**

So, when someone says, *"You've got good energy,"* they're not just being polite. They're sensing something real.

You're constantly radiating a measurable field, whether you realize it or not.

Invisible Signals

We're all walking around with invisible vibrations shaped by our thoughts, emotions, and intentions.

It's not about being perfect.
It's about being **present.**

Because the more aligned you are inside, the more your energy speaks for you — without a single word.

YouTube Break
"You ARE Energy" – Dr. Joe Dispenza

Dr. Dispenza explains how your thoughts and feelings create a vibrational signal — and that signal shapes your future experiences.

He says:

***"You don't attract what you want.
You attract what you are."***

That's the key.
Not just what you *wish for* when you're calm, but what your energy is constantly saying underneath the surface.

Belief = Vibration

Let's take two people. Both say:
"I believe I can change."

- **Person A** says it with doubt, shoulders slouched, stomach tight.
- **Person B** says it with a calm breath, chin up, eyes intensely clear.

Same words. Different frequency.
And the world responds to that energy.

Why Alignment Matters
This is why affirmations don't always work.

If your body is still vibrating with fear while your mouth says, *"I love myself,"* then your energy and your words are sending two different messages.

The goal is **alignment.**

- When your beliefs match your emotions…
- When your emotions fuel your actions…

- When your inner world and outer choices agree…

That's when your energy becomes undeniable.

True Transformation

When your **mind believes it, your heart feels it, and your body carries it**, that's alignment.
Not forced. Not faked. But embodied.

It's the moment everything inside you agrees: *"I'm ready."*
Because true transformation doesn't come from willpower alone.

It comes from wholeness — when your thoughts, emotions, and actions begin walking in the same direction.

That's not just growth.
That's **becoming.**

Real-Life Example: Meet Lacey

Lacey was nine months into recovery.
Clean. Committed. Consistent.
She went to her meetings.
She journaled every day.

She even taped affirmations on her bathroom mirror:
- "I am healing."
- "I deserve happiness."
- "I am enough."

But nothing felt different.
She still felt like a fake —
Like someone pretending to be okay.

Then one day, her therapist asked:
"Do you feel those affirmations in your body?"
That question hit hard. Because the answer was no.

She said the right things...
But she still carried tightness in her chest.
Still clenched her jaw.
Still flinched when given a compliment.
Her energy hadn't caught up to her words.

So, she tried something new:
- She visualized the "worthy" version of herself
- She played music that felt like joy
- She walked with her shoulders back, feeling strong
- She practiced breathing into confidence

And after a few weeks... Something started to shift.
Not because the world changed.
But because her vibration did.

But here's where it gets even more powerful: once Lacey began to feel her affirmations in her body, her outside world started shifting too. People began treating her differently because she was finally radiating it. She walked into rooms with her shoulders back and her eyes soft, and people mirrored that energy right back to her.

***She noticed that when she spoke to others, her words carried more weight — not because she forced confidence, but because she embodied it. It wasn't about pretending. It was about practicing until her nervous system got the message:* this is who I am now.**

Let's Talk Frequencies
Every emotion you feel isn't just psychological — it's vibrational.

Your emotions carry a frequency, a measurable energetic signal that affects your body, your environment, and even your outcomes.

You've probably felt it before:
- *Love has a light, expansive feeling.*
- *Fear feels heavy and tight.*
- *Joy lifts your whole body.*
- *Shame sinks you like a stone.*

That's because emotions are energy in motion (e-motions), and that energy vibrates at different rates.

The Frequency of Emotions
Based on the research of Dr. David R. Hawkins, here's a simplified emotional frequency scale — measured in units of vibration (Hz):

BELIEVE. BEHAVE. BECOME.

Emotion	Vibration Level	Description
Enlightenment	700–1000	Unity with all
Peace	600	Spiritual presence
Joy	540	Gratitude
Love	500	Compassion, connection
Reason	400	Logic, understanding
Acceptance	350	Trust
Willingness	310	Empowerment, optimism
Pride	175	Arrogance, defensiveness
Anger	150	Frustration,
Guilt	30	Blame, unworthiness
Shame	20	lowest vibration

Think of this scale like a staircase. You don't jump from the basement of shame to the rooftop of enlightenment in one leap — you climb, step by step. And that's okay. If you're in anger today, that's already a higher vibration than guilt. If you can shift from anger to courage, you've already changed the entire frequency of your future.

Recovery isn't about living at the top of the scale all the time. It's about recognizing where you are and reaching for the next step. Over time, those steps compound into a very real, very lasting transformation. That's how you rewire your life — not by pretending you're already at joy, but by faithfully moving upward, one vibration at a time.

Why It Matters
These aren't just abstract numbers. They reflect how you experience reality:

- At lower frequencies (like shame or guilt), you feel stuck, powerless, and disconnected.
- As you rise (into courage, love, and joy), your energy field expands — and life opens up.

This isn't just spiritual lingo — it's bioenergetics. It's quantum physics. It's recovery science.

The Good News
Your frequency isn't fixed. You can learn to shift it — moment by moment — by changing:

- Your thoughts
- Your breath
- Your focus
- Your self-talk
- Your environment

You don't have to force joy. Just reach for one level higher.
From shame to guilt.
From guilt to grief.
From grief to courage.
And eventually, to love.

Sound & Frequency in Healing
Music heals.

You've felt it — one song lifts you up, another breaks you open. That's not an accident.

Sound = vibration. Vibration = energy.

Here's a simple way to experience this:
Close your eyes. Take a slow breath in. As you inhale, imagine pulling in the vibration of a sound that lifts you — maybe a favorite song, maybe a healing tone like 528 Hz.

Feel the way your chest expands as the sound moves through you. On the exhale, imagine releasing the vibration of whatever has weighed you down.

Many in recovery use healing frequencies during:
- Meditation
- Journaling
- Emotional resets
- Inner child work
- Sleep routines

This isn't imagination only — your body is literally tuning to the vibration you focus on. That's why people describe certain music as cleansing or uplifting. You're not just hearing it, you're absorbing it. Each inhale is an invitation to harmonize with a higher frequency. Each exhale is a chance to let go of the static that's kept you stuck.

YouTube Break:
"528 Hz Frequency – The Love Vibration"

The 528 Hz frequency is often called the "miracle tone." It's linked to DNA repair, heart-healing, and emotional balance.

Try it before a meeting.
Try it when you feel anxious, stuck, or disconnected.
Let the sound reset your frequency.

Practice: Matching the Energy

Words:
"I'm healing."
Ask:
"Do I feel peace in my body when I say that?"

Words:
"I deserve love."
Ask:
"Can I say it without flinching? Or breathe deeper when I speak it?"

If not — don't force it.
You're not broken.
You're just re-aligning.

Try this instead:
Close your eyes
Picture what it would feel like if it were true
Soften your breath
Smile gently, even just a little

You're not pretending.
You're practicing a new energetic truth.

Belief Frequency Check-In

Step 1: Choose Your Belief
Pick one belief you're actively working on.

Example:
"I am worthy of love."

Step 2: Say It Out Loud
Now speak your belief. As you do, tune in to your body. Pay attention to:

Your voice – Is it steady or shaky?
Your breath – Deep or shallow?
Your gut – Calm or tense?
Ask yourself:
Do I feel expansion or contraction?
Does my body open up or shut down?

Step 3: Embody the Belief
Ask: *"What would this belief feel like if it were completely true?"*

Now visualize the version of you who truly lives it:
- How do they walk?
- What's their tone of voice?
- What music do they listen to?
- How do they move through a room?
- How do they respond to compliments?

Bring that version of you to life — even just for a moment.

Step 4: Anchor the Feeling
Choose a physical anchor to help lock in the frequency:
- A song that matches the emotion
- A scent (lavender, peppermint, etc.)
- A color that resonates with your belief

- A breathing rhythm that makes you feel calm

Use your anchor daily to re-enter the feeling state.
Let your nervous system learn it.
Let your cells memorize it.

Final Reminder:
Belief isn't just about convincing your mind.
It's about training your whole body to agree.

Your Body Is an Antenna
Every single day, you're broadcasting a signal — even when you're silent. That signal isn't based on what you post online, or what you say in public...

It's based on what you believe deep down —
the thoughts you think when no one's watching.

So, if you keep finding yourself in:
- Toxic friendships
- Unfulfilling jobs
- Cycles of self-sabotage

It's not because you're broken.
It's not fate.
It's a frequency issue.

Your signal just needs a reset.
Ask Yourself:
- "What is my energy saying about me?"
- "Is my signal based on love or fear?"
- "Does it invite growth or protect me from it?"

The moment you shift your belief,
your breath,
or your focus...

Your **signal** *begins to change. And when your signal changes — everything around you will respond.*

Behavior Alignment Tracker

Why Track Behavior?
What you do is a reflection of what you believe.
This isn't about perfection — it's about closing the gap between your intention and your action. Let's track if your behavior matches the version of you that you're becoming.

STEP 1: Define Your Identity Goal
Fill in the sentence below:
"I am a person who..."

Examples:
- ...keeps promises to myself
- ...protects my peace
- ...walks in love, not fear

Your chosen identity is your compass. It sets the direction for how you move, speak, think, and respond — especially when life gets loud. The clearer you are about who you're becoming, the easier it becomes to align your choices with that truth. Every aligned action is a vote for your transformation.

STEP 2: Daily Alignment Check-In
For the next 5 days, reflect on one key behavior each day.

Key Behavior Examples:
- The way I talked to myself
- How I handled a trigger
- Whether I followed through
- How I showed up in group
- How I treated someone I care about

STEP 3: Alignment Reflection

What patterns do you notice this week?
When did you feel most aligned? What were you doing right?
When did you feel off? What threw you off?
What can you shift this week to realign with your identity?

Behavior Loop Awareness
When you catch yourself drifting, walk through this:

Trigger – What set me off?
Thought – What did I say to myself?
Behavior – What did I do next?
Alternative – What aligned response could I try next time?

Bonus Practice: Walk It Back

"That action didn't match who I'm becoming.
I'm walking it back — and trying again with love."

You don't have to be perfect.
You just have to notice — and redirect.

Every time you "walk it back," you're rewiring your energy. Instead of letting old patterns lock in, you interrupt the cycle and teach your nervous system a new response. That tiny pause is not weakness — it's strength. It's proof you're becoming more conscious of the energy you carry.

Personal Reflection

When I first entered the nonprofit sector, I had a lot to learn about professionalism. Within my first few months at *The Davis Direction Foundation*, I nearly found myself in several physical altercations.

The environment was filled with newcomers, and everyone was still working on their "attitudes." Guess who else was still working on his? Having my CEO admonish me in front of my co-workers was humbling, but it served its purpose.

I realized I was demanding a level of respect that I wasn't giving. If someone got loud with me, I matched their energy. If they held a grudge, I held mine longer. But deep down, I knew that wasn't who I wanted to be, so I had to work on it.

I couldn't expect to be taken seriously if anyone could push my buttons. I was reacting like the old me while looking for results that belonged to a more mature version of myself.

Learning how to track behavior — then adjust it — is empowerment. Each time I reacted negatively toward a client, it was old programming surfacing. But the version I was working to manifest was slow to anger in every form.

To grow, I had to learn how to observe my behaviors, then correct them. That process allowed me to become who I knew was inside. Now you have the same process in your hands — and you can apply it when you're ready.

Final Thought:
At the end of the day, beliefs aren't just words in your head — they're signals in your body. They shape how you stand,

how you breathe, how you respond, and what you radiate into the world.

Thoughts alone can come and go like clouds. But once a thought fuses with feeling, it becomes energy. And energy always moves — outward into your relationships, inward into your habits, and forward into the future you're building.

This is why your work isn't to "think positive" and hope for the best. Your work is to **align the thought with the feeling** until the two become one. Because when your belief is embodied — when your mind, heart, and body agree — the energy you emit is undeniable.

CHAPTER FIVE

Faith Isn't Blind, It's Creative

It's 6:12 a.m. You're staring at your shoes by the door. Part of you says, "Not today." Another part whispers, "Just ten minutes." Faith lives in the moment your hand reaches for the laces. That is the beginning of momentum.

We've been told that faith is something you have —
like a possession you either carry or lack.
But what if faith is something you do?

> **"Faith is taking the first step, even when you don't see the whole staircase."**
> — *Dr. Martin Luther King Jr.*

What if faith is a muscle — one you build, flex, stretch, and strengthen through movement?

Faith isn't about being fearless.
It's about moving anyway.

Courage isn't the absence of fear. It is the decision that something else matters more. In recovery, that "something" is your future. It's not about having every answer. It's showing up with a whisper of belief and a handful of courage.

Faith Is Not Wishful Thinking
Many of us were taught to wait:
- Pray hard
- Hope for change
- Sit still, just in case we mess it up

But that's not faith.
That's **fear** *in disguise.*
Real faith?
It moves.
It builds.

It speaks up in meetings.

It paints the first stroke when the canvas still looks blank.

Let's Pause...
If you're reading this, there's a part of you that already knows the following:

Hope says:
"Maybe one day it'll get better."

Faith says:
"I'm building that day now."

You don't need perfect faith to begin.
Just enough to take the next step.

The Formula
Belief + Emotion + Action = Creation

This is the code behind every transformation — past, present, and future. Once you understand it, you can use it on purpose.

Belief – The thought you choose to focus on
Emotion – The energy that fuels it
Action – The movement that activates the vision

When these align, they create momentum.

Example: *Belief* — "My voice matters." *Emotion* — a steady breath and a calm chest. *Action* — raise your hand and share for sixty seconds. Result — a micro-win that teaches your brain this is who you are now.

Neuroscience tip:
When belief, emotion, and action line up, your brain enters coherence — a peak state for healing, learning, and rewiring.

Small, purposeful movements increase dopamine and norepinephrine, chemicals that sharpen focus and increase motivation. Your mood often follows your movement.

A belief with no emotion is just theory.
A belief with no action is just a wish.
You want change? Add movement.

Let's Talk About Noah (Yes, that Noah)
Whether you view the Bible literally or symbolically — Noah's story is about creative faith.

God tells Noah a storm is coming.
But there are no clouds.
No thunder.
No rain in the forecast.

Still, Noah builds the ark.
People mock him.
Call him crazy.

But Noah builds anyway — based on faith, not evidence.
That's not just belief.

That's alignment with possibility.

Today's ark might look like a resume sent after ten rejections, a phone call to make amends, or showing up to a meeting when no one promised to meet you there. Build before the weather changes, and you'll be happier for it.

YouTube Break:
"The Power of Movement – Steven Furtick"

"Sometimes you don't get the feeling of faith until after you move."
— *Pastor Steven Furtick*

You won't always feel ready.
But when you take the step anyway, your energy shifts.
You become what you couldn't reach by standing still.

Your Brain Responds to Movement
The First Five Minutes Protocol: When you feel stuck, do five minutes only. Five minutes of walking, writing, cleaning, or studying. Momentum is built in minutes, not marathons.

Ever feel better after:
- Making your bed?
- Taking a walk?
- Showing up to group, even when you didn't want to?

That's dopamine at work — your brain's way of saying:
"We're not stuck anymore."
"We're choosing life."
"We're building something different."

Even when:
Your hands shake
Your voice cracks
Your heart still doubts
Faith is about moving through fear.

JEFF VICKERS
Story in Action: Meet Shana

Shana had a vision:
- Become a peer support specialist
- Speak in schools
- Mentor young women

But the inner voice said:
"You're not ready."
"You need to fix more first."
"Who are you to lead?"

Her mentor told her:
"Faith doesn't wait for perfect.
Faith moves like it's already on the way."

So, Shana:
- Studied old workbooks
- Practiced her story in the mirror
- Sat front row at workshops
- Volunteered
- Applied for her first certification

She didn't wait for confidence.
She created it.
Now?

Her first talk lasted four minutes. Her hands shook. Two girls stayed after and said, "Thank you." She's leading her first support group and mentoring others. That was the proof her fear could not give her.

BELIEVE. BEHAVE. BECOME.
The Neuroscience of Acting "As If"

Behavioral Activation is a clinical tool that means:
Do the thing you want to become — even if you don't feel ready for it yet.

Want to *feel* like a leader? **Act** like one.
Want to *feel* confident? **Stand** like it.
Want to *feel* worthy? **Show up** like you are.

Why it works:
Every time you behave like the person you're becoming, your brain builds new neural pathways.

Over time:
- Confidence becomes normal
- Courage becomes natural
- Action becomes identity

YouTube Break:
"Fake It Till You Make It? – Dr. Andrew Huberman"

Dr. Huberman explains:
"Even if your mind isn't fully on board,
your body can lead the way."

Repeat the action.
Train the brain.
Change the life.

Creative Faith Blueprint
A practice to put faith into motion — not just as a feeling, but as a creative force.

Step 1: Pick a Vision
What do you want to become or create?
- "I want to lead a meeting."
- "I want to be a better parent."
- "I want to start a podcast."
- "I want to go back to school."
- "I want to rebuild trust with my family."

Be honest. Be bold.

Step 2: Write One Belief That Supports It
a. "I have something valuable to say."
b. "I'm growing into the parent I needed."
c. "I have the courage to learn something new."

Let this belief become your mental anchor.

Step 2.5: Set a cue in your environment
Place an object in view that sparks this belief. A lock-screen phrase, a sticky note on the bathroom mirror, or a bracelet you touch before you act.

Step 3: Anchor It with Emotion
Ask yourself:
"What emotion would this version of me feel?"

Would they feel:
- Confidence?
- Gratitude?
- Excitement?

Close your eyes.
Take a deep breath.
Feel it in your body.

Step 4: Take One Aligned Action Today
It doesn't have to be big, but it does have to be real. Try:
- Writing a personal mission statement
- Making a phone call you've been putting off
- Reading one article about your goal
- Practicing your story
- Submitting an application
- Watching a video that lights you up
- Sitting down to plan the next 7 days
- Tiny moves create massive momentum.

Common blockers: *fatigue, overthinking, fear of judgment.*

If-then plans:

- If I'm tired, then I will do two minutes and stop.
- If I start overthinking, then I will write one sentence and hit send.
- If I fear judgment, then I will tell one safe person and act anyway.

Remember This:
Faith isn't waiting on the sidelines, crossing your fingers, hoping the moment feels right. Faith suits up and walks like it already made the team.

Faith doesn't ask for permission.
It doesn't wait for proof.

It doesn't need every step mapped out in advance.
You're not pretending. You're not playing make-believe.

Faith moves like the vision is already unfolding —
because on a deeper level, it already is.
You're training your nervous system
to recognize the truth of what's possible.

And every time you take a step — even when your hands shake, even when your voice trembles — you're laying down the bricks of the bridge between who you used to be and who you are becoming.

Personal Reflection

A few years ago, I had an experience that reshaped my understanding of faith.

While working as a lead facilitator, I was arrested and spent twelve days in jail for crimes I had committed during active use. Strangely, I didn't feel fear.

By that time, I had a strong relationship with my Higher Power, and I refused to believe I would serve time. My mind believed I had already atoned for my past, and my heart was fixed on freedom.

Over those twelve days, I was moved to three different jails. During that time, I focused on my affirmations and chose to see myself happy and free. I believed my faith would free me. If I rested in His love and refused to cower in the face of adversity, He would free me — and He did.

That was my first experience of *intentionally practicing faith*. When I apply that moment to the steps outlined here, it's clear how I approached it:
Step 1: I picked a vision of freedom.
Step 2: I believed in my atonement.

Step 2.5: Seeing anyone happy became my visual cue.
Step 3: Feeling the joy of my desire kept me motivated.
Step 4: I repeated my affirmations verbally.

That was the first time I truly realized that faith the size of a mustard seed can move a mountain. Beyond believing in the outcome, our aligned actions must carry personal power.

In that moment, my affirmations became the alignment. I believed those affirmations. They were statements of power and resonance I had repeated for three years. I had no idea I would one day walk through three jails reciting them, like Joshua circling Jericho.

After hearing them for so long, my brain wired itself to believe them — and my body produced the chemistry to reinforce those beliefs.

***

This isn't **fantasy.**
This is **neuroplasticity.**
This is **spiritual alignment.**
This is how identity rewrites itself.
And that future version of you?

They're already standing on the other side, hands cupped around their mouth, cheering you forward like your life depends on it — because it does.

Emotional GPS Mapping Tool

Why Map Emotions?

Emotions don't just "happen." They're not random. They're intelligent signals sent by your nervous system to help you navigate life.

Think of emotions like notifications on your phone — they pop up for a reason. Not to annoy you, but to inform you. To wake you up. To show you what's going on beneath the surface.

Most of us were taught to suppress them, fix them, or hide them. But when you learn to feel your emotions instead of fear them, they transform from roadblocks into road signs.

They become a built-in GPS — pointing you toward the parts of yourself that are asking to be seen, healed, or honored.

Because when you understand the message, you can choose the response — instead of reacting on autopilot.

Let's explore how to read that map.

STEP 1: Identify Your Default Emotional Setting

When life gets hard, which emotion tends to drive the wheel?

Observe which applies:
- Anger
- Shame
- Guilt
- Anxiety
- Numbness
- Fear
- Loneliness
- Control
- Avoidance
- People-pleasing

Other: _____

STEP 2: The Last Time I Felt This Way
Reflect on a recent emotional moment:

What happened?

What emotion came up?

What story did I tell myself in that moment?

What did I do next (reaction)?

Did this response serve me or sabotage me?

What response would feel more aligned with who I'm becoming?

STEP 3: Rewire the Pattern — Pause, Feel, Reframe
Every emotion has a story — and most of us respond without realizing we're repeating old patterns. To change that, we practice three key steps:
- **Pause** — When something triggers you, stop for a moment. Take a breath before reacting.
- **Feel** — Acknowledge the emotion that's rising. Don't push it away. Don't judge it. Just feel it.
- **Reframe** — Ask yourself:
  "What's my usual reaction here?"
  "Does that reaction reflect who I'm becoming?"
  "What's a new response that feels more aligned with the version I'm growing into?"

Example:
Trigger: Someone criticized your idea in group.
Emotion: Embarrassment + defensiveness.
Old Reaction: Shut down, withdraw, or snap back.
New Aligned Response: Thank them for their input.

Remind yourself that one opinion doesn't define your worth.

STEP 4: Build Your Emotional Vocabulary
Sometimes we feel "off" but can't pinpoint why.

Use this list to get more specific:
Instead of "angry," am I actually...
- Frustrated
- Disrespected
- Overwhelmed
- Afraid
- Ignored

Instead of "sad," am I really...
- Lonely
- Disappointed
- Hopeless
- Misunderstood

Write your top 3 "go-to" emotions and what they usually mean in your life:

_____ = Usually means:
_____

_____ = Usually means:
_____

_____ = Usually means:
_____

The better you name it — the better you can navigate it.

BELIEVE. BEHAVE. BECOME.

STEP 5: Emotional Check-In Log (3 Days)

For the next three days, take a moment each evening to check in with your emotional state. Reflect on the following prompts to better understand your patterns and build emotional balance:

Day 1
What emotion was most present today?
What triggered that emotion?
What kept you grounded/what made things harder?

Day 2
What emotion was most present today?
What triggered that emotion?
What helped you stay grounded/what made things harder?

Day 3
What emotion was most present today?
What triggered that emotion?
What helped you stay grounded/what made things harder?

Use this log to build emotional awareness, track shifts in your mood, and identify what supports or sabotages your inner peace. You're learning to respond, not just react.

YouTube Break:

"Emotional Release & Soothing Frequencies – 432Hz + 528Hz"

Use this as background music while journaling, or calming your nervous system.

Final Reminder:
Your emotions are not enemies.

They are messengers — wise, ancient signals from your
nervous system trying to get your attention.
Every emotion you feel carries information.

It's not weakness.
It's data.
It's feedback.
It's truth.

And now that you've learned how to listen —
how to name, feel, and navigate your inner world —
you don't have to stay stuck in old loops.
Because now?

You've got a compass.
You've got a map.
You've got the tools.

Faith is the way your future borrows your feet.

CHAPTER SIX

Your Emotions Are Guidance Systems

JEFF VICKERS
Let's Talk About Feelings

Yeah — those things we're taught to:

- Hide
- Numb
- Ignore
- Pretend don't exist

In early recovery, most of us learn how to stop using.
But almost no one teaches us how to start feeling.

And yet...

Emotions are not the problem.
They're the signal.
They're not the enemy.
They're the messenger.
They're your internal compass — always pointing toward something your mind may have missed.

The question isn't:
"Why am I feeling this?"

The better question is:
"What is this feeling trying to tell me?"

Most slips start as a feeling we didn't name in time. When you spot and name the wave, you create a gap between urge and action—and in that gap, you get to choose.

Feelings Are Messengers

Think of emotions like the notification system on your phone.

- Anger might say: "Your boundaries are being crossed."
- Fear might say: "Something feels unsafe — pay attention."
- Sadness whispers: "It's time to let go or grieve something real."
- Shame screams: "You've forgotten your worth — come home to it."

We've spent most of our lives deleting these notifications before we read them. We weren't taught emotional literacy — we were taught emotional avoidance. Every time we ignore emotion, we ignore truth.

Try this new belief on:
"My feelings don't make me weak. They make me aware."

> **Emotion vs. Story**
> *Sensation*: tight chest
> *Emotion*: fear
> *Story:* "I'm not safe"

What Happens When You Ignore Signals?

You already know this — because you've lived it.

When we don't deal with emotion, it doesn't disappear. It transforms into something heavier:

- Sudden outbursts, shutdowns, silent treatments
- Addictions: substance, control, chaos, perfectionism
- Chronic pain, tightness, insomnia, fatigue

Avoided emotion becomes trapped energy.
That energy will come out — through your health, habits, or through your relationships.

True recovery isn't just about not using.
It's about learning how to feel — and listen.

If avoiding emotion has been your survival strategy, here's a lens that can help you understand why.

YouTube Break:
"How to Feel Your Feelings – Gabor Maté

> Dr. Maté says:
> *"The question is not 'Why the addiction? 'The real question is: 'Why the pain?'"*

Pain ignored becomes pain repeated.
But pain acknowledged becomes pain released.

Emotions Are Not Proof You're Weak

Feeling deeply doesn't mean you're broken — it means you're awake. Awake to your truth. Awake to what matters. It means your heart hasn't gone numb, even after everything you've been through. In a world that teaches us to shut down, your sensitivity is proof that you're still alive, still open, still capable of healing.

But many of us were taught:

- "Crying is weakness"
- "Real ones don't feel"
- "If you show emotion, you'll get played."

So, we learned to:

- Shut it down
- Numb it out
- Turn it into rage, control, or silence

That's not strength — that's survival mode.
It served you once, but healing is a new game.
In healing? Emotion is essential.

Real Life: Meet Devon

Devon grew up hearing:

- "Stop being soft."
- "Man up."
- "Tough it out."

By 12, he hid all emotions.
By 16, he numbed with weed.
By 22, heroin.

In treatment, a counselor told him:
"You've been taught to fear your emotions — but they've only ever been trying to help you."
That changed everything.

Devon started seeing:

- Anger = boundary alarm
- Sadness = time to slow down
- Fear = a warning, not a prison

Now? He runs with his feelings — like a GPS guiding him forward.

Iris

Iris used to treat guilt like a verdict, disappearing for days whenever she made a mistake. In group, she learned to translate it as, "repair is needed," not "I am bad." She sent a simple text—"I own what I did and want to make it right"—and her body finally exhaled. Now guilt cues action, shame cues self-compassion, and both become bridges back to connection instead of traps.

Emotions Move Through the Body

Emotion = energy in motion. They're meant to move — not stay stuck in any one place.

If they don't move, they can show up as:

- **Grief** → chest tightness
- **Anxiety** → stomach knots
- **Anger** → jaw tension
- **Stress** → back pain

Dr. Bessel van der Kolk, *The Body Keeps the Score*:
"Unfelt emotions don't disappear. They store themselves in the body."

You don't need to fix the emotion.
You need to feel it — and let it move through.

Practice: Feel → Name → Move

1. **Feel It**
   Pause and notice the sensation. No story. Just sensation.
   Say: "I feel something moving in me."
2. **Name It**
   Naming an emotion lowers its intensity.
   "This is sadness."
   "This is shame — and I am safe to feel it."
3. **Move It**
   - Journal it
   - Talk to someone
   - Walk/stretch
   - Deep breathing
   - Cry, yell, dance

BONUS TOOL: The Emotional Guidance Scale

(Adapted from Abraham-Hicks)

Use this scale to track and gently shift how you feel:

- Joy / Empowerment / Love
- Passion
- Enthusiasm
- Hope
- Contentment
- Boredom
- Frustration
- Overwhelm
- Anger
- Blame
- Guilt
- Shame / Powerlessness

Don't jump from Shame to Joy.
Just move one level at a time.
Even a slight shift changes your chemistry.

To turn this awareness into change, try a simple 3-day Emotion Log. Jot quick notes after charged moments—what happened, what your body did, the emotion you named, the action you chose, and how you felt afterward. In a few days you'll start to spot patterns (what triggers you, what helps you regulate) and can adjust sooner next time.

Suggested columns:
Date | Trigger | Body | Emotion | Action | After-feeling

Tip: Keep it in your phone's notes or your journal; each entry can take 1–2 minutes.

Message in the Emotion

Step 1: Recall a recent emotional moment.
Example: You felt angry when someone ignored your boundaries.

Step 2: Ask:
"What was the message in that emotion?"
Examples:

- "I felt disrespected."
- "I wanted to feel safe."
- "This reminded me of something old."

Step 3: Reflect:
"What could I do next time instead of numbing or reacting?"
Options:

- Breathe
- Journal
- Use "I feel" statements
- Walk away
- Ask for clarity

Use these simple I-statements right after you identify the message in your emotion. Keep them short, and specific.

1. **Behavior boundary**
   I feel [emotion] when [specific behavior]. I need [clear need]. Are you willing to [specific request]?
2. **Time/space boundary**
   I feel [emotion] when [pressure/expectation]. I need [time or space]. Are you willing to [alternative or plan]?
3. **Communication boundary**
   I feel [emotion] when [tone/words]. I need [respectful, calm conversation]. Are you willing to [speak later/take a 10-minute break/]?

Personal Reflection

Learning to regulate my emotions has changed how I relate to my mother.

There was a time resentment ran the show. If we argued, I'd explode. Recovery gave me enough calm to look underneath. I can hold empathy for her history and the shame she still carries—and still tell the truth about what hurt.

Our relationship is better, and we still hit the same snags. She's in her early 70s. When I name that she often prioritizes other people's feelings over mine, she doesn't always understand. Her version: *"You got the short end of the stick."*

My version: **she and my stepdad abandoned me, so I had to move in with her mother, and growing up, I was repeatedly molested.** Those facts still shape what safety means to me.

Every so often, she tries to mend fences with my stepdad and uncle. Recently, she asked me to invite both to my wedding. I've already attempted repair over the years; an invitation would have cost my peace on a day that must be safe. To her, *inclusion* mattered; to me, **protection** mattered.

I used *regulation + boundaries*. I named the message in my emotion and spoke an I-statement:
"I feel dismissed and unsafe when I'm asked to include people connected to my harm. I need my wedding to be a protected space. Are you willing to drop this topic with me?"

She didn't receive it the way I hoped. (This was not the first instance. I've repeated this over the years to her. I reminded her of this and expected her to say that she remembers and wouldn't do it again.)

Old me would have cursed, hung up, and stayed angry for days. Instead, I repeated the boundary once, stated the consequence, and followed through: **"If this comes up again, I'll end the conversation."**

She has 23 years in recovery. She is still emotionally limited in some ways. Both can be true. I can love her and stop abandoning myself.

Regulation didn't change her response. It changed mine. It kept me aligned with who I'm becoming.

The lesson I've learned is that boundaries are how I choose connection without self-betrayal; I don't **need** agreement from others, but I do need consistency on my part; and love can be honest, firm, and calm at the same time.

Closing Truth

You are not "too emotional."
You are deeply alive in a world that often teaches us to numb, silence, or shrink.

Your emotions are not flaws — they are frequencies. The way your nervous system signals safety or threat. They are signals from the soul, trying to guide you home to yourself.

Recovery doesn't mean shutting down.
It doesn't mean pretending nothing hurts.
It means building the capacity to feel everything
...without being controlled by it.

That's emotional wisdom —
And it doesn't come from avoiding your pain.
It comes from listening to it, gently, until it transforms.

And that wisdom?
It's already in you.

So let yourself feel.
Let yourself learn.
Let yourself rise —
One feeling at a time.
One breath at a time.
One truth at a time.

SECTION TWO

BEHAVE

(CHAPTERS 7-10)

BELIEVE. BEHAVE. BECOME.

CHAPTER SEVEN

Your Body Hears Everything Your Mind Says

JEFF VICKERS
Let's Start with a Simple Truth

Your body is always listening.

It listens when you speak out loud.
It listens when you talk to yourself.
It even listens when you don't say a word — but you think it.

Every thought you have becomes a message.
Every belief becomes a broadcast.
Every word, whether whispered or screamed inside your head, becomes a signal your body picks up.

The question is:
What kind of messages are you sending?

Because just like a child listening to a parent, your body listens closely — and it believes you.

It's 10:42 p.m. You're rinsing a glass at the sink. A thought slips in: "You blew it again." Your shoulders drop. Your jaw tightens. Breath turns shallow. No one else said a word. Your body heard you and reacted.

You pause, palm on the counter. You say—quietly—"I'm safe. I'm learning. I can repair this." Your chin lifts. Shoulders ease back. Breath lengthens. The knot in your stomach loosens, heartbeat steadies, warmth spreads through your chest. Nothing outside changed. Only the message did.

That's the mind–body conversation happening all day. Your words are cues; your chemistry responds. Let's learn to send messages that heal.

The Mind–Body Connection Is Real

Science has proven it.
Spiritual teachers have taught it.
People in recovery live it daily — often without realizing it.

Here's what that means:
- When you're anxious, your heartbeat changes.
- When you're ashamed, your immune system weakens.
- When you constantly think "I'm a failure," your brain and body adjust their chemistry to match that belief.

This connection between thought and health isn't just "positive thinking talk" — it's biology.

The official name for it?
Psychoneuroimmunology — the science of how your thoughts affect your nervous system, immune system, and overall well-being.

Science Snapshot:
How a Thought Becomes a Body Feeling

A thought starts in your mind, your brain treats it like a cue, and your body follows.

Thought → Brain signal → Hormone/nerve changes → Immune and gut effects → Felt experience.

Example: You think, *"This meeting will go badly."* Your brain flags threat, breathing shifts shallow, cortisol bumps up, heart rate climbs, blood flow leaves your gut (hello, stomach churn), and your immune system goes into short-term defense mode.

Nothing "happened" yet—just a thought. Change the thought ("*I can handle this; one step at a time*"), and the brain sends a different signal: breath deepens, tension eases, digestion settles, and your system returns toward balance.

Let's break that down:
- Psycho = Your thoughts and beliefs
- Neuro = Your brain and nerves
- Immuno = Your immune system
- Logy = The study of how it all works together

Your thoughts don't stay in your head.
They echo through your body — like ripples in a pond.

Thought-to-Body Loop
Thought / Belief → Emotion → Body Sensation → Behavior → Result → Reinforces Belief

Quick example:
"I'm going to mess this up" → anxiety → tight chest, shallow breath → avoid the task → deadline pressure grows → ***"See? I always mess up."***

How to use it:
Spot where you are in the loop and change one link (thought, breath, or action) to shift the outcome.

Real Talk for Recovery
If we're honest, most of us in recovery have spent years sending our bodies toxic messages:
- "I'm worthless."
- "I hate myself."
- "I'll never change."
- "I don't deserve peace."

Maybe we didn't speak those words out loud.
But we thought them.
We felt them.
We believed them.

And guess what?
Our bodies responded — not with logic, but with chemistry:
- Chronic tension
- Inflammation
- Tight muscles
- Panic attacks
- Insomnia
- Sickness we couldn't explain
- Fatigue we couldn't fix

We weren't just physically exhausted.
We were emotionally malnourished.

But here's the good news: **Just like the body believed the bad messages, it can believe the good ones, too.**

If strong affirmations trigger resistance, try these gentler truths that move you toward self-kindness:
- I am open to being kinder to myself.
- I am learning to respect my body.
- I can practice gentle words today.
- I am willing to see myself with softer eyes.
- I can be on my own side, even a little.
- I am doing the best I can with what I have.
- I can let today be easier than yesterday.
- I am practicing speaking to myself like I care.
- I can choose one caring action for my body today.
- I am willing to believe peace is possible for me.
- I am learning to notice harsh self-talk.
- I can allow progress to come in small steps.

Mini Check: Spot Your Pattern
1. Which two or three symptoms show up for you most often?
2. When do they spike? Note times, situations, people, or places.
3. What were you saying to yourself right before they spiked?

Tip: Jot your answers in the margin or notes. Look for repeats this week.

YouTube Break:
"The Biology of Belief – Dr. Bruce Lipton"

In this powerful talk, Dr. Bruce Lipton — a stem cell biologist — explains how your beliefs shape your biology even more than your DNA does.

He says:
"Your cells are listening to your thoughts.
Change the signal, and you change the outcome."

Translation:
Positive self-talk isn't cheesy — it's cellular nutrition.
What you say to yourself doesn't just change your mood — it changes your entire internal environment.

Here's a Chemistry Cheat Sheet:
- Supportive — dopamine — calm focus
- Supportive — serotonin — steadier mood
- Supportive — oxytocin / endorphins — connection
- Stress — cortisol — tight chest, wired-but-tired
- Stress — adrenaline — racing heart, shallow breathing

Let's Break Down the Signals
Every thought you think releases chemicals.

Here's a simple breakdown:
Hopeful thoughts → *Dopamine, serotonin, endorphins*
These help you feel calm, motivated, creative, clear-headed. They boost your immune system and help the body repair.

Fearful or shameful thoughts → *Cortisol, adrenaline*
These prepare your body for danger — even when there is none. They keep you stuck in "fight, flight, or freeze." Long-term, they can damage your heart, gut, memory, and sleep.

Think of your body like a garden.
Your thoughts are the water.

If you water it with fear, self-hate, and shame — what kind of fruit will it bear?

But if you water it with gentleness, hope, and encouragement...
Healing begins to grow.

Here's what changing the internal broadcast looked like for one person.

Story in Action: Meet Tina
Tina used to wake up every day thinking:
1. *"I hate myself."*
2. *"I'm disgusting."*
3. *"What's the point in trying?"*

She didn't need anyone to insult her — she was already doing it, almost from the moment she woke up. When her brain "booted up," those "programs" started to run... Honestly, they were already running "in the background." Her waking up just made her conscious of them.

And her body responded:
- Daily migraines
- Irritable bowel syndrome (IBS)
- Heart palpitations
- Night sweats
- Fatigue so heavy she could barely stand on some days

Then, in trauma therapy, something shifted.

Her therapist asked:
"Would you speak that way to a child you love?"

Tina broke down crying. Because deep down, she knew:
She had become her own bully.

So, they started small:
"I'm healing."
"My body is doing the best it can."
"I deserve kindness — even from myself."
"Peace is possible."

At first, it felt fake. But over time?

Her panic attacks eased. Her gut calmed down.
She started smiling — and meaning it
She didn't change overnight.
But she changed the conversation — and her body listened.

Ty
For years, Ty woke with a clenched jaw and near-daily afternoon headaches. After two weeks of practicing softer self-talk—"I can learn," "I'm safe to try"—he noticed he was unclenching at night. By week four, the headaches dropped

from daily to once a week, and his breathing felt easier during the day. Nothing else in his routine changed; the conversation inside did, and his body followed.

Mirror Work: Your Words Matter
Louise Hay, a pioneer in self-healing, taught a practice called mirror work — the act of speaking kind, healing truths to yourself in the mirror.

It might feel awkward at first.
You might laugh. Cry. Resist it.

But it's powerful — and backed by brain science.

Studies show:
Self-affirmation activates the brain's reward centers. This helps rewire old trauma loops and create new pathways of trust and safety.

Interestingly, I've been fond of speaking into mirrors for years. Back in active use, I'd glare into mirrors and rap, sing, or say anything self-deprecating. Without realizing it, I was using negative affirmations to reinforce how I viewed myself.

Flash forward to 2020, when Ms. Angela (my counselor) introduced me to a handheld mirror from the dollar store. My assignment was to take 5 minutes a day and positively affirm who I was becoming. Oh, and I had to look into that mirror the whole time!

Talk about feeling uncomfortable. At first, I couldn't stand it. **I avoided eye contact with myself.** My brain didn't believe my words, nor did my body, at first. But slowly, I began to change. Over time, my brain coded my affirmations and sought patterns to reinforce my words. Then my body yielded and believed. That's when I "embodied" the truth.

Something amazing happens when we speak love to ourselves while observing ourselves. These days, I enjoy listening to my personalized affirmations while looking in a mirror and doing a light workout. Even if you haven't started exercising, you can still apply yourself...

Try this:
Stand in front of a mirror. Look into your own eyes.
Say (*slowly, even if you don't believe it yet*):
  1. "I am not my past."
  2. "I'm proud of how far I've come."
  3. "My body is healing. My heart is opening. I am safe now."

Do it once a day for 7 days.
Notice how you feel — in your body and your spirit.

The Nervous System Wants Safety
Your nervous system has one main question it's asking all day long. If you start listening, you'll agree.

The question is:
"Am I safe?"

It listens for the answer through:
  o Your tone
  o Your posture
  o Your breathing
  o Your inner dialogue

When you speak to yourself gently, your nervous system says: **"Yes, we're okay."**

But when you criticize yourself harshly, it hears:
"We're under attack."

The brain responds by triggering stress hormones — even when there's no external danger. Healing can't happen in a body that feels unsafe. That's why speaking kindly to yourself is one of the most powerful healing tools you'll ever use.

Quick Safety Reset Menu
When your system asks, "Am I safe?" give it a clear yes. Try one of these for 30–90 seconds:

• Physiological sigh
Inhale through your nose, take a second small sip-in, then a long, slow exhale through your mouth. Repeat 3–5 rounds. This pattern signals your body to downshift out of threat.

• Humming
Gently hum any tone for 60 seconds, mouth closed or slightly open. The vibration and long exhale help settle your heart rate and calm the nervous system.

• Hand on chest + longer exhale
Place your palm at the center of your chest. Inhale for a count of 3, exhale for a count of 4–6. A longer exhale cues safety and steadies your breath.

• Cold water splash
Run cool water over your face, wrists, or the back of your neck for about 30 seconds. Brief cold exposure can nudge your body toward a calmer state.

Use these before mirror work, hard conversations, cravings, or whenever the inner critic gets loud. Pick one and practice daily so your body recognizes it fast.

JEFF VICKERS
Rewriting the Internal Script

Let's walk through this step-by-step.
Step 1: Listen In
What's one negative thing you've been telling yourself?
Example: *"I always mess everything up."*
Be honest. Write it down.

Step 2: Name the Impact
How does that belief make your body feel?
Example: *"Tight chest, shallow breath, heavy arms."*
Awareness helps you track the damage.

Step 3: Flip the Script
What's a kind, believable reframe?
Try: *"I get better with every mistake."*
Make it something your heart can almost believe — and practice from there.

Step 4: Repeat It Daily
Say it in the mirror.
Write it on sticky notes.
Whisper it while brushing your teeth.
Let it become your new inner soundtrack.

7-Day Evidence Log
Each night, list three tiny proofs that you acted from your new script today. Small counts. Examples: answered a text you were avoiding, took a breath before speaking, chose gentle words, went to bed on time, did two minutes of breathwork, drank water while repeating your affirmation.

Day 1

BELIEVE. BEHAVE. BECOME.

Day 2
_____

Day 3
_____

Day 4
_____

Day 5
_____

Day 6
_____

Day 7
_____

Week-end reflection:
What pattern did you notice?
_____
Which cue, or phrase helped most?
_____
Where will you double down next week?
_____

***

Why This Matters (Even to Your Cells)
Your body is made up of nearly 60–70% water — and every word you speak becomes a signal to that water.

Some readers experience the water practice as spiritual symbolism, others as motivation science—use what's helpful and safe for you.

Dr. Emoto, a Japanese researcher, famously photographed frozen water crystals that were exposed to words like "love" or "hate."

The **"love"** crystals formed beautiful, harmonious shapes.
The **"hate"** crystals were jagged and chaotic.

His message?
Water responds to energy.
That's not poetry — it's physics.
Every sound, thought, and intention carries a frequency.

And since your body is made up of nearly 70% water, those frequencies don't just pass through you — they shape you.
After discovering Dr. Masaru Emoto's work, my mindset shifted. I understood the basics of affirmations, but watching the many "Rice Experiment" videos on YouTube changed how I practiced them.

People around the world—and later, several of my own cohorts—repeated a simple test inspired by Emoto's ideas about water and memory: identical jars of cooked rice are spoken to with different intentions. Over time, the rice appears to reflect the energy it receives.

In that framework, the water within the cooked rice is the change agent. Intention—carried by words—imprints on the rice (which is mostly water). Because water "remembers" energy, that imprint becomes visible, much like the patterns seen in frozen water.

For the last three years, I've recorded my affirmations as MP3s and played them to my drinking water. I treat it like music: the water holds the message, and every swallow is an upload.

These days I also add specific crystals and mineral salts to further "charge" the water while the affirmations play. The results for me have been tangible: I haven't had a common cold in years, my skin looks great, and most days feel great.

This is the science and soul of self-talk:
Affirmations aren't cheesy.
They're cellular commands.
Your biology is listening.
Make sure what it hears supports your healing.

YouTube Break:
"Self-Love Affirmations | 528 Hz Healing Frequency"

This music blends self-love affirmations with healing sound frequencies.

Play it while:
- Journaling
- Driving
- Falling asleep
- Cleaning
- Sitting in silence

Let the words and sounds begin reprogramming your nervous system — gently, layer by layer.

Bonus Practice: Charge Your Water with Intention
Your body is mostly water — and water responds to energy.

Before you drink your next glass, try this:
Hold the glass in your hands.
Speak your affirmation aloud:
"I am safe. I am healing. I am loved."

Take a slow breath and visualize those words entering every cell. Then drink — as if you're drinking in the truth.

This simple act turns hydration into healing.
Because when you speak life over your water, you speak life into yourself.

If you do not have time: On rushed days, speak your affirmation into your palm (quietly or in your mind), place that hand on your chest for three slow breaths, then drink the water you already poured. Your hand carries the intention, your breath signals safety to your nervous system, and the ritual stays simple and consistent.

Reminder:
The words you speak to yourself shape the world inside your body.

They affect:
- Your heart rate
- Your hormones
- Your digestion
- Your energy
- Your confidence
- Your ability to rest, recover, and heal

If you've spent years at war with yourself,
Let this be the year you make peace.

Start with a whisper:
"I'm proud of how far I've come."
"I'm safe now."
"My body hears me — and we're healing together."

BELIEVE. BEHAVE. BECOME.

Because your healing doesn't just live in your mind.
It lives in your words.
In your nervous system.
In your cells.
And every kind word is a seed. Plant it.
Water it. Let it grow.

Personal Reflection

I have a relationship with my water, and I'm not ashamed to say it.

When I say that, I don't mean I worship a glass. I mean I use hydration as a daily ritual to regulate my nervous system and practice speaking life. People joked in 2023 about "talking to your water." I smiled—I've been doing a version of that since 2021.

I first met the idea through Dr. Masaru Emoto and the many "rice experiments." Some see them as symbolism, others as science. Either way, the lesson landed for me: attention and intention change outcomes. That insight didn't just shift how I talk to water—it changed how I talk to myself.

When I facilitated at New View Wellness, we ran a simple version in group. Folks felt silly at first, then noticed how the *act* of slowing down, breathing, and choosing kinder words softened their bodies. That was the point: our words are signals the body hears.

So now my routine is simple, not mystical:
Fill a glass. Hand on heart. One slow breath.

Speak one line I'm practicing:
"I am safe. I am healing. I am loved."

Sip slowly, like I'm drinking in the truth.

Sometimes I add trace minerals, a little hydrogen, soft music, or set a carafe near light and a few crystals. Nice, not necessary. The medicine isn't the props—it's attention + hydration + breath + language, all pointed in the same direction.

The goal used to be "stay hydrated." The goal now? Create a daily moment where belief becomes behavior, and behavior becomes biology. I don't just drink water—I practice with it. Breathe. Bless. Sip. Align.

If *"water memory"* isn't your thing, keep the ritual anyway. Your nervous system understands slow breath, kind words, and steady sips—and your day will, too.

Reward Habit Builder

Why This Matters
Your brain is wired to repeat what feels good. This means one of the fastest ways to create new habits in recovery is to connect small actions with emotional rewards.

We're going to build a system that gives your brain proof that change feels good — not just scary.

STEP 1: CHOOSE A MICRO-ACTION
Pick one small, consistent behavior you want to build over the next 7 days:
- Something that supports your recovery
- Takes less than 10 minutes
- Can be done anywhere

Examples:
1. Text a peer for support
2. Do 2 minutes of breathwork
3. Read one paragraph from this book
4. Stretch or move your body
5. Journal 3 sentences

My Micro-Action:
"Every day, I will _____."

STEP 2: CHOOSE A REWARD
Pick one healthy, meaningful reward you'll give yourself right after completing the action.

It doesn't have to be big or expensive — just something that feels good to your body, calming to your mind, or satisfying to your heart.

The key is consistency. When your brain begins to associate effort with positive emotion, habit change becomes easier. This reward should feel nourishing — something that tells your nervous system: "Well done. That mattered."

Examples:
• Listen to your favorite song — really feel it
• Sip your favorite tea or coffee slowly
• Step outside and look at the sky or touch a tree
• Light a candle or use a calming essential oil
• Say something kind to yourself in the mirror — and mean it
• Do a happy dance, stretch, or take a deep breath of relief

My Reward:
"After I complete the action, I will
_____."

Reward Ladder
To keep rewards effective and build consistency, level them up over three weeks.

Week 1
Give yourself the chosen micro-reward every time you complete the action.

Week 2
Use the same reward only when you complete the action two days in a row.

Week 3
Swap to a non-food, non-screen reward. Examples:
- Step outside for two minutes of fresh air
- Take a hot shower or bath
- Listen to one favorite song with full attention
- Do a gentle stretch or short walk
- Make a cup of tea and sit in silence for five breaths

Notes:
Keep rewards immediate. Pair them within five minutes of the action so your brain links effort to feeling good. If you miss a day, simply resume at the current week. This is about momentum, not perfection.

If I Miss a Day
Do this to keep momentum and avoid all-or-nothing thinking:

1. Write one self-compassion sentence: "It's okay to be human. I'm back now."
2. Do the micro-action for 60 seconds right now.

3. Check the "Did I Reward Myself?" box to reinforce the loop.

No penalties. Resume tomorrow and keep going. Consistency grows from returns, not perfection.

STEP 3: HABIT TRACKER (7 DAYS)

Day	Did I Do the Action?	Did I Reward Myself?	Mood Before	Mood After
Day 1	Y/N	Y/N		
Day 2	Y/N	Y/N		
Day 3	Y/N	Y/N		
Day 4	Y/N	Y/N		
Day 5	Y/N	Y/N		
Day 6	Y/N	Y/N		
Day 7	Y/N	Y/N		

Tip: Be honest with yourself. This isn't about being perfect — it's about noticing what builds momentum.

STEP 4: IDENTITY INTEGRATION

Now that you've completed (or attempted) 7 days:
What did this teach me about myself?
_____
_____

What version of me does this habit belong to?

"This is what a _____ does."
Example: "This is what a grounded woman in recovery does."

Every thought you think is a message.
Every word you whisper to yourself is a command.

And your body?
It listens. Closely:

- When you tell yourself, "I can't," your shoulders curl.
- When you say, "I'm not enough," your chest tightens.
- When you repeat, "I'm safe now," your breath deepens.
- Your body doesn't argue with your thoughts — it adapts.

It shifts its chemistry, posture, and rhythm to match the story your mind is telling. This is why affirmations are more than nice words. They are instructions.

They teach your body how to feel — how to be.
So today, speak to yourself like someone worth healing.
Talk to yourself like someone worth loving.
Because you are.
And your body is always listening.

CHAPTER EIGHT

Behaving Like The Future You

"You don't become what you want. You become what you believe and behave." — **Oprah Winfrey**

You're standing at the sink after another long day. Your phone lights up with an invite you know leads nowhere good. For a breath, you hover between old you and new you. This is where the future isn't later—it's your next choice.

Let's get straight to it.
You say you want to be free.
You say you want to change your life.
You say you want to become someone new.

That's beautiful.
That's sacred.
That's possible.

But here's the hard — and powerful — truth:
You can't just wait for that version of you to arrive.
You have to start behaving like them now.
That version of you you dream about?
They're not waiting in the future.
They're waiting in your next choice.

Who Are You Becoming?
Take a moment. Close your eyes if you need to.
Picture the version of you you're becoming — the one who has:
- Peace of mind
- Healthy boundaries
- Strong routines
- Joy that isn't dependent on anything external

Friendships that feed your spirit.
A job that aligns with your values.

BELIEVE. BEHAVE. BECOME.

A deep sense of worth and purpose.
Freedom from chaos, shame, and addiction.

Now ask yourself:
- What does that version of you do on hard days?
- How do they talk to themselves after a mistake?
- What do they do when no one is watching?
- How do they show up when they're triggered?
- How do they respond when their buttons are pushed?

Most people wait until they feel like that future version before they act differently.

But real transformation starts with this question:
"How can I start doing what they would do — today?"

Even if you don't feel like them yet.
Even if you're scared.
Even if your voice shakes and your hands tremble.
Do the thing anyway.

You Don't Fake It. You Practice It.

Pretending: hides, performs, needs approval.
Training: repeats, learns, doesn't need perfect feelings.

Some people hear this and say:
"So I'm just supposed to fake it till I make it?"

No. You're not faking anything.
You're practicing something new.
Pretending hides your truth.
Training honors your growth.

Just like someone in the gym isn't pretending to be strong — they're building strength. Same goes for you.

1. You don't have to "believe" it all the way.
2. You don't have to "feel ready."
3. You just must start behaving in alignment with who you're becoming.
4. You behave your way into belief.
5. You move your way into mindset.
6. You act like it's true — until your body, brain, and behavior begin to agree.

If I feel the urge to bail, **then** I text my sponsor and take a 90-second walk.
If I make a mistake, **then** I say, "Repair beats retreat," and send one honest message.
If I wake up foggy, **then** I do my 60-second breath + one tiny task before coffee.

Here are a few "self-talk swaps":
"I don't feel like it → I'll do two minutes."
"This won't matter → Reps wire identity."
"I already blew it → Returns build resilience."

Story in Action: Meet Tony

Tony got clean, but every day still felt like survival.

He was free from using — but still stuck in old habits.
He wanted more.
He dreamed of launching his own landscaping business.
He wanted to be a provider. A mentor. A man of peace and purpose.

But every time something went wrong — a no-show client, a flat tire, a late payment — the old Tony came out:

BELIEVE. BEHAVE. BECOME.

- Yelling
- Blaming
- Quitting
- Escaping

Until one day, his sponsor asked:
"What would future Tony do right now?

The version who already owns the business and lives that life?"

Tony paused.
Breathed.
Put down the blame.
Texted his customer with professionalism.
Put on his boots.
Finished the job.

That moment didn't look flashy.
But that was the day he started living as his future self — not just in theory, but in behavior.
That's when the shift began.

YouTube Break:
"Acting Like the Person You Want to Be – Mel Robbins"

Mel Robbins explains how change happens not through "waiting to feel different," but by acting your way into new identity.

She says:
"You have to stop waiting to feel like the future you — and start moving like them."

Every step you take in alignment with that vision?
It teaches your brain:
"This is who we are now."

Brain Science

Your brain doesn't change because of what you know.
It changes because of what you do — over and over.

This is called **self-directed neuroplasticity** — your brain's ability to rewire itself based on repeated behavior.

Here's the breakdown:
1. Repeat anxious thoughts? → Your brain builds anxious pathways.
2. Repeat peaceful actions? → Your brain builds calm pathways.
3. Repeat boundary-setting? → Your brain makes confidence easier next time.
4. Repeat discipline? → Your brain makes follow-through more natural.

And the best part?
Your brain doesn't need you to believe 100%.
It just needs you to take the next aligned action.

Even a 1% shift in behavior changes your neural map.
The new you isn't born in a lightning bolt of motivation.
The new you is shaped in the next 5 minutes.

Most urges crest and fall within minutes—stack two future-you actions inside that window and you outlast the wave.

Snapshot: Repeated actions fire the same neural circuits. What fires together, wires together. Each rep lays a little more myelin on the path. Tomorrow's "hard thing" becomes 1% easier because today you walked the path.

Anchoring Into Identity
Identity is who you believe you are.
Behavior is how you prove it to yourself.

So, try this. Ask yourself:
1) "What does the me I'm becoming do when they wake up?"
2) "How do they eat, move, rest, and talk to themselves?"
3) "What do they tolerate? What do they walk away from?"
4) "What do they post, read, wear, prioritize?"
5) "What energy do they carry into a room?"

Now — don't try to change everything at once.
Pick just one behavior that matches that identity.
Start there.

- Posture: soften shoulders, lengthen spine.
- Breath: 4-count inhale, 6-count exhale before speaking.
- Gaze: meet eyes for two seconds, then relax.
- Pace: move 10% slower than your urge—calm leads.

Let that one behavior become your anchor —
The bridge between who you've been and who you're becoming.

Future You Embodiment Map
Step 1: Name the Identity
Who are you becoming? Say it clearly.

- "I'm a sober, present parent."
- "I'm a calm, consistent leader."
- "I'm a business owner in recovery."
- "I'm a woman of peace and purpose."
- "I'm a man who chooses love over fear."

Step 2: List 3 Daily Actions That Person Would Take
For example:
- Wake up at 7 a.m.
- Speak respectfully even under stress
- Plan the day the night before
- Respond to texts calmly
- Prioritize rest
- Journal emotions instead of stuffing them.

Step 3: Start With One Today
Don't wait until Monday.
Don't wait until you "feel" like it.
Don't wait for a sign.
Do it now. Even imperfectly.

- Place water + journal by the bed.
- Set your lock screen to your identity sentence.
- Pre-start a "focus" playlist.
- Put a 3×5 "One Thing Today → _____" card on the fridge.

BELIEVE. BEHAVE. BECOME.

Filled Example: Future You Embodiment Map

Identity: "I'm a calm, consistent leader. "Three daily actions:

1. Take a 2-minute breathing reset before every call.
2. Send a gentle agenda text the night before meetings.
3. Keep my phone off the table during meals and 1:1s.

Today's one action:
Send the agenda text for tomorrow's check-in.

Every single time you act like the future version of you, your brain rewires around that identity.

Mini Habit = Major Identity Shift
Let's say your future-self meditates each morning.
Start with 30 seconds. Seriously.

Why?
Because it's not just about the habit — it's about the identity confirmation.

- Future You reads every day? → Start with one paragraph.
- Future You sets boundaries? → Start with one "No" today.
- Future You eats clean? → Start with one better decision at lunch.
- Future You leads meetings? → Practice introducing yourself differently.

You're not trying to "arrive" overnight.
You're training your brain to recognize:
"This is who we are now."
That's where momentum is born.

Here are two techniques you can implement:

- **2-Minute Rule:** Do the first 120 seconds only. Stop if needed.
- **Bundle:** Pair a hard task with a wanted cue (coffee only while journaling three sentences).

Group / Meeting Integration Cards
Future-You Introduction (30 seconds)

- "Today I'm practicing being a _____ (identity: e.g., calm, consistent leader).
- One action I'll take in the next 24 hours is _____.
- If you see me slipping into _____ (old pattern), please nudge me with: 'Breathe and choose.'"

Two-Minute Check-In Prompts

Use these three quick prompts for shares or partner check-ins:

- **Win:** One action I took that matched my future self.
- **Wall:** One moment I defaulted to an old pattern.
- **Next 24:** One specific action I'll take before tomorrow.

60-Second Reset Before You Share

- **Posture:** Uncross legs/arms, feet on floor, shoulders soft.
- **Breath:** Two gentle inhales through the nose, long slow exhale through the mouth.

BELIEVE. BEHAVE. BECOME.

- **Phrase:** Silently say, "I can choose who I am, even now."
- **Pick one:** Name the next tiny action your future self would take.

YouTube Break:

"I Am Affirmations." 432 Hz Manifestation Loop

Play this while:
- Walking
- Cooking
- Journaling
- Cleaning
- Falling asleep

Let the rhythm and repetition begin to shape your inner dialogue. Let it help your nervous system relax into the version of you that's already becoming.

Personal Reflection

Having a vivid imagination as a child helped a lot with the loneliness. It was programmed out of me through chaos in my life.

Thankfully, I'm tapped back into that divine internal technology. I'm grateful for the teachings on visualization from Drs. Joe Dispenza and Robert J. Gilbert.

When I started this journey, the practice was simple: train my attention to see what I was building—mental rehearsal. Seeing is the first level of mind–body mastery. I picked one image and held it. When my mind wandered, I brought it back—no drama, just reps. Everything else was noise.

Over time the picture sharpened. With enough mental rehearsal I could run a three-scene loop in my mind's eye: the beginning (how I enter), the middle (how I move through challenge), and the end (the outcome). Once the 'mind movie' was memorized, I moved to the next phase: embodiment—bringing the vision from head into body.

As I ran the scenes, I practiced the state they carried: excitement, awe, love, joy. When my physiology matched the picture, it became real to my nervous system. From there, the work was simple, not easy: condition my body to trust those states and return to them on cue.

First, I trained my mind to see the future; then I trained my body to believe it. Daily reps kept me living from that future—thoughts, breath, and behavior aligned—until the gap between 'there' and 'here' collapsed into the only place change happens: **NOW**.

And when doubt visits (because it will), I run a 60-second reset: shoulders back, two soft inhales and a long exhale, replay the end scene, feel one emotion on purpose, then take one tiny, aligned action within five minutes. That's how visualization stops being an image and becomes a way of moving through the day.

Final Truth of This Chapter
You don't become someone new by waiting for proof.

Speak like your future self — even if your voice shakes.
Move like your future self — forget the old story.
Choose like your future self — even if your hands tremble.

Because the fastest way to become them...
is to act like them now.

CHAPTER NINE

Reclaiming Play, and Creativity

You're standing at the sink after another long day. The room is quiet except for the faucet and your own tired breathing. You try to remember the last time you laughed without forcing it—and come up blank. A simple question arises: *"When did I stop doing anything just because it felt good?"*

When was the last time you felt *light?*
Not just clean.
Not just sober.
Not just surviving.
But *light-hearted*.

Curious.
Playful.
Free.

If it's been a while — you're not alone.
In recovery, we're often taught how to:
Stay grounded
Stay focused
Stay clean
Stay committed

And yes — all of that matters.
But let's not forget... Your aliveness.

You Were Born Creative

Every child is born knowing how to:
- o   Make up stories
- o   Pretend the floor is lava
- o   Ask "Why?" a hundred times
- o   Make silly noises
- o   Sing out loud with zero fear of judgment

That used to be you. You used to be fearless in your imagination. But then...
Trauma said:
- "Be quiet."
- "Stay small."
- "Grow up fast."

Addiction said:
"We don't have time for joy."
"The only thing that matters now is relief."

Suddenly, imagination seemed pointless.
Play felt childish.
Joy felt out of reach.

But here's the truth most people miss:
Creativity isn't just for kids or artists.
It's for humans.

And one of the most powerful healing forces around. Whether you paint, dance, build, write, rap, sew, or freestyle —it's not about being good at it.
It's about being alive in it.

YouTube Break:
"The Power of Play – Brené Brown on Joy & Vulnerability"

In this clip, Dr. Brené Brown explains how play is not just a luxury — it's medicine for people who've lived in shame, fear, or survival mode.

She says:
"Play is the opposite of depression.
It's the birthplace of connection, innovation, and joy."

You don't grow out of the need to play.
You grow back into it when you heal.

Why Play Matters (Science Snapshot)
Play isn't extra—it's regulation. Low-stakes, joyful activity shifts your nervous system from threat to safety, which is the state where learning and healing happen.

It tends to boost feel-good neurochemistry (dopamine, endorphins, oxytocin), lowers stress signals, and wakes up flexible, creative networks in the brain. Practiced regularly, play improves focus, emotional regulation, and decision-making—the same skills recovery asks of you.

Real Talk: Recovery Can Feel Heavy
Let's be honest.
Sometimes recovery feels like:
- Homework
- Schedules
- Rules
- Steps
- Meetings
- Boundaries
- Responsibility
- Always doing it "right"

That's important — structure brings safety.

But here's the other side of the coin:
1) You didn't come here just to avoid relapse.
2) You came here to live.

And living includes:
- Laughing until your stomach hurts

- Making things just because you want to
- Asking questions nobody can answer
- Dancing in the kitchen with no rhythm
- Writing wild stories or silly poems
- Singing off-key
- Creating something just to do it

Recovery without joy is still just another prison.
You were not born to be a robot — but to feel again.

Quick Play Audit
Circle how often each is true for you this month:
Never / Rarely / Sometimes / Often

1. I laughed so hard my body loosened.
2. I made something just because I wanted to.
3. I moved my body playfully (danced, stretched).
4. I lost track of time in a healthy, creative way.
5. I asked "What if...?" and followed the curiosity.
6. I made silly sounds with zero judgment.
7. I invited someone else to play with me.

Score yourself by counting "Sometimes" (1) and "Often" (2).
0–3: Your play system needs fuel. Pick one and schedule it this week.

4–7: You're warming up. Bump one from "Sometimes" to "Often."

Goal for this week: Choose one line above and plan a 10–20-minute version of it.

Story in Action: Meet Deja

Deja spent years numbing her pain behind substances, silence, and striving for perfection.

She didn't laugh.
She didn't rest.
She didn't play.
She got clean, but her life felt... gray.
No chaos. **But no color either**.

Then one day at a women's group, someone brought out paints and markers. Deja rolled her eyes and thought:
- *"I don't do art."*
- *"I'm not a kid."*
- *"I'm not here for arts and crafts."*

But something inside her — that quiet voice — asked her to stay for a while.

She picked up a brush.
Started with a swirl.
No plan. No pressure. Just color.
She painted a messy, wild canvas.
In the middle, she wrote one word: "Hope."

She smiled — for real — for the first time in months.
Now?
Every Sunday, she paints.
Not to sell it.
Not to prove anything.

Just to reconnect with a part of herself that addiction buried — but never destroyed.

Micro-Success Story: Ten Minutes of Play
After treatment, Ari felt numb and "too serious" all the time. She tried a 10-minute "play window" every evening: one song to dance to, a messy doodle, or a photo walk in her apartment. By week two, the heaviness started to lift; by week four, her sleep and mood had noticeably improved. Her takeaway: "I didn't need talent. I needed permission."

Creativity Heals the Brain
Let's talk science.

Being creative is one of the most underrated natural techniques to stay healthy. When you engage in creative activities — like drawing, dancing, writing, or singing — your brain releases:

- Dopamine → boosts motivation and pleasure
- Serotonin → stabilizes mood
- Oxytocin → deepens feelings of connection
- Endorphins → reduce stress and physical pain

And more than that?

Creative expression strengthens the prefrontal cortex — the part of your brain responsible for:
- Focus
- Emotional regulation
- Impulse control
- Decision-making

Which means...
When you play, you're not just having fun.
You're rewiring your brain for recovery.

It's not selfish.
It's not a waste of time.
It's medicine.

Curiosity Is the Compass

Creativity doesn't ask for perfection — it asks for permission.

To explore.
To wonder.
To try things just for the hell of it.

Curiosity is the compass that leads us back to ourselves.
Shame says:
1) "You're not creative."
2) "You're too old."
3) "You'll look stupid."
4) "That's not recovery work."

But curiosity whispers:
- "What if you are?"
- "What if you tried anyway?"
- "What if this is the healing?"

***

Creative Confidence Bridges
If "I'm creative" feels too far away, try bridge statements that your body can believe:

• I'm open to experimenting with no-pressure creativity.
• I can give myself five minutes to play without judging it.
• I'm learning what lights me up again.
• I'm willing to try, even if it's messy.
• My curiosity counts, even when the product doesn't.
• I don't have to be good at this to benefit from it.

BELIEVE. BEHAVE. BECOME.

Pick one bridge for the week and repeat it before you start any playful activity.

In recovery, we unlearn the belief that everything must be earned through pain. Joy can be medicine.
So can laughter.
So can play.

Practice: Your Play Menu
Let's make this tangible.

Right now — without judgment — list 10 things that feel:
1. Light
2. Creative
3. Curious
4. Playful
5. Joyful

They don't need to be deep.
They don't need to be useful.
They just need to be you.

Here are some sparks to get you going:
a) Doodle with crayons
b) Dance barefoot in your living room
c) Try on funky outfits
d) Make a playlist of songs you loved at 10 years old
e) Sing badly on purpose
f) Take funny selfies
g) Garden in silence
h) Bake without a recipe
i) Write a letter to your future self

Now circle one. And do it this week — **no matter what**. Not to heal. Not to achieve.
Just to remember what it feels like to feel.

7-Day Play Starter

Keep it tiny and consistent. Set a daily 5–10 minute "play window" this week. Use the same time each day if you can.

Day 1: Put on one song you loved as a kid and move however you want.
Day 2: Doodle lines, shapes, or patterns without lifting the pen for five minutes.
Day 3: Step outside and list ten details you notice (colors, textures, sounds).
Day 4: Free-write one page that begins with "Today I'm curious about…"
Day 5: Build or arrange something small (blocks, spices, books, leaves).
Day 6: Make a three-photo mini-story on your phone that captures "joy."
Day 7: Share one tiny creation (or the story of doing it) with a safe person.

Reflection prompt: What felt easiest? What surprised you? What do you want more of next week?

The Inner Artist Isn't Dead — Just Dormant

Here's a truth you weren't told:
- ◊ You don't need to be an "artist" to be creative.
- ◊ You just need to be human.

Every human creates.
It's how we process.
How we breathe spirit into the world.

So, if you've been living gray —
If the color got stripped from your days —
If the spark got buried under rules and regret —
This chapter is your permission slip.

Not just to recover.
But to rediscover.
Your joy.
Your spark.
Your art.
Your self.

The Imagination Mirror

Grab a journal.
Or stand in front of a mirror.

Ask yourself:
1. What did I used to love before the pain started?
2. What would 7-year-old me beg me to do today?
3. Where did I hide my joy when I stopped feeling safe?

Then, just write. Or move. Or play.
However, it wants to come out — let it.
You are not too far gone.
You are not too old.
You are not too broken.

You are still in there.
And she, he, or they?
Are ready to play again.

Joy & Play Menu
Theme: Reclaiming Play, Curiosity, and Creativity

Recovery isn't just about avoiding relapse — it's about rediscovering your aliveness:

- Joy isn't a luxury.
- Play isn't childish.
- Creativity isn't optional.

They are medicine.
And they belong to you.

STEP 1: BUST THE LIES
Let's get real, we're all still working on toxic beliefs, so which of these have you carried (in your mind and body)?

I don't have time for fun.
I have to earn joy.
Being silly makes me look weak.
Creativity is for "artsy" people — not me.
If I stop grinding, I'll lose momentum.

Which one hits hardest and why?

STEP 2: BUILD YOUR JOY & PLAY MENU
Create your personal "menu" of light, curious, creative activities. No rules. No pressure. Just stuff that sparks something in you. Use any that fit—or add your own:

5-Minute Sparks
- Doodle lines and shapes on scrap paper
- One-song dance break in the kitchen
- Step outside and name five colors you see

- Hum or sing one chorus out loud

15–30 Minute Play
- Paint or finger-paint a messy page, no plan
- Free-write two pages without stopping
- Take 10 quick photos of textures or shadows
- Bake or cook without measuring
- Learn three guitar chords or a simple drum pattern

With Someone
- Play cards or a board game
- Cook a simple meal together
- Library visit and pick a random book by its cover
- Sidewalk chalk with a child or neighbor
- Call a friend and swap made-up stories

Outside
- Cloud watching or star spotting
- Barefoot in grass for two minutes
- Slow walk while naming every sound you hear
- Sketch a tree or building you like
- Pick up ten pieces of litter on your block

Make/Build
- Collage from old magazines
- Fold origami or paper airplanes
- Build something small with blocks or scraps
- Start a jar herb garden
- Curate a 10-song "joy playlist"

Curiosity Prompts
- Ask one question no one can answer
- Try a new route home and notice three details
- Do a daily task with your non-dominant hand
- Write a tiny poem about what you see right now
- Learn one fun fact and teach it to someone

Add Your Own

_____

_____

***

Habit-Stacking (Play + Something You Already Do)
Attach a playful act to an existing routine so it happens:

• After brushing teeth → hum one full chorus.
• While coffee brews → doodle lines and shapes.
• After you park → snap one "texture" photo.
• Before a shower → 60-second stretch or silly dance.
• While dinner simmers → write three curious questions.

Pick one pair and run it for seven days. Now circle ONE thing for this week — not for a goal... but for your soul.

STEP 3: PLAYFUL IDENTITY CHECK-IN
Ask yourself:

Who was I before the world told me to grow up, toughen up, or shut up?

_____

_____

What did I love doing as a kid — just for fun?

_____

_____

What might my inner child still want to explore?
_____
_____

STEP 4: CREATE YOUR "NO JUDGMENT" ZONE

Write out a permission slip to yourself.

I give myself permission to:_____.

Even if:
1. I look silly
2. Nobody claps
3. I'm not "good" at it
4. It doesn't make money
5. I have no clue what I'm doing

Because:
My healing includes joy.
My creativity is valid.
I deserve to feel alive again.

Brain Science

When you play, your brain releases:
- Dopamine (motivation + joy)
- Oxytocin (bonding + connection)
- Serotonin (mood regulation)
- Endorphins (natural painkillers)

This isn't just cute — it's neuroscience for recovery.

JEFF VICKERS
Personal Reflection

One of my blessings in recovery is JOY. Not the fireworks kind. The everyday current that runs beneath whatever feelings move through the day.

Joy showed up when I stopped bargaining with my past and started keeping tiny promises to my present.

I used to beg for "something" and, once it arrived, talk myself out of wanting it. I did that with jobs, with people, with things. Recovery broke that loop. It taught me to stay.

The self-discovery this path gave me is joy I won't trade. In chaos or a trigger, I sometimes forget—but clarity returns: breathe, name what's true, choose the next right move.

If I weren't in recovery, I wouldn't have the "normal" problems I have now—
rent, schedules, hard conversations, showing up on time.
I'd have crisis problems.
I'm grateful for the ordinary ones.

That's how I measure progress:
fewer emergencies, more choices;
less chasing, more presence;
a quiet joy that keeps pace with me all day.

Final Truth

Joy is not a bonus for later.
It is a vital sign of your healing now.
Play is not childish.

BELIEVE. BEHAVE. BECOME.

It is how your nervous system remembers safety, curiosity, and possibility. **Creativity is not about talent.** It is about breath, color, sound, and movement returning to your life.

You do not have to earn this.
You do not have to apologize for this.
You were born with it.
It is still in you.
Let it out.

Before You Turn the Page
1. Choose one tiny spark from your Play Menu.
2. Put it on tomorrow's calendar for five minutes.
3. Say out loud: "Joy counts here."
4. Do it whether or not you feel ready.

A Note for Hard Days
If today feels heavy, make play gentle and close to the body: one song, one stretch, one color on a page, one deep breath at an open window. Tiny still rewires.

Remember
Recovery is not only the absence of chaos.
It is the presence of color.
It is laughter returning to the room.
Keep reaching.
Keep creating.
Keep becoming.

CHAPTER TEN

You Are Not Broken
You Are Becoming

You're standing at the sink after another long day.
The old voice whispers, *"You're still broken."*

You pause, hand on the counter, and hear a quieter one beneath it: ***"I'm not broken. I'm becoming."***

Water off. Shoulders soften. For the next five minutes, you choose to treat yourself like that's true.

Settle In.

Let's slow down for a second.
Take a breath.
Let it land…

- You've come a long way in these pages.
- You've questioned the stories you were handed.
- You've looked at your beliefs.
- You've learned how your brain works.
- You've started speaking kindness to yourself.
- You've practiced being the person you want to be.
- You've dared to dream of joy again.

That's not small.
That's sacred.

- You've peeled back layers that didn't belong to you.
- You've stood face-to-face with your patterns.
- You've taken steps others said were impossible.

And now comes the most important truth of all:
You are not broken.
You are becoming.

Identity drives behavior. Most slips happen when the 'I'm broken' story takes the mic. Naming 'I'm becoming' gives you one more beat to choose differently.

Quick Proof Audit (this week)

Tiny win #1: _____
Tiny win #2: _____
Tiny win #3: _____

Receipts matter. *Naming them teaches your brain,* ***"This is who we are now."***

The Lie of "Broken"

The world may have told you:
- "You're too far gone."
- "You'll never change."
- "You're damaged goods."
- "You blew your chances."

You might've even whispered it to yourself after a relapse, a mistake, a rough night:
"I'll never get it right."
"There's something wrong with me."
"I can't come back from this."

But none of that is true.
You are not broken —
You've just been through a lot.

And sometimes surviving can leave dents that look like damage but are really signs of resilience.

BELIEVE. BEHAVE. BECOME.

There is a difference between:
- Being shattered and being shaped.
- Being lost and being between identities.
- Being wounded and being in process.

There's nothing wrong with being in process.
Butterflies don't look like butterflies when they're becoming.
Sometimes we mistake becoming for being broken.

Here's another truth:
⇒ Your pain shaped you — but it doesn't define you
⇒ You get to decide what it becomes.

Nature Doesn't Rush — It Transforms

Look at the natural world.
Nothing rushes, yet everything changes.

A seed doesn't bloom overnight. It cracks. Breaks open.
Disappears underground before it ever grows upward.

A caterpillar literally digests itself — turning to liquid before it transforms into a butterfly.

It melts before it flies.
A diamond is just carbon under pressure.
Coal plus time, plus stress, plus unseen transformation.
That's the process…

You are in process, too.
Transformation takes time.
It's messy.

It's invisible for a while.
But *it's always happening* underneath the surface.

If it feels slow...
If you're not seeing results yet...
If your old self is still trying to pull you back...

It doesn't mean you're failing.
It means you're becoming.
And becoming takes more than one season.
It takes grace.

YouTube Break:
"The Power of Yet – Carol Dweck on Growth Mindset"

Psychologist Carol Dweck explains how the word "yet" changes everything:
"I don't have it... yet."
"I'm not there... yet."
"I don't fully believe in myself... yet."

That's growth.
That's hope.
That's becoming.

Meet Isaiah: Becoming in Real Time
Isaiah relapsed after 8 months clean.

He felt crushed.
Devastated.
Embarrassed.

He told his sponsor, "I blew it. I'm back at square one."
He thought the relapse erased all his progress.
He thought he had failed again.

But the sponsor paused and said something Isaiah never forgot:
"Relapse doesn't erase recovery. It just shows you where your healing still has roots to grow."

That hit different.

Isaiah wasn't broken.
He was still on the path.
Still learning.
Still becoming.

He started seeing relapse not as the end, but as a signal:
- Where do I need more support?
- Where did I forget who I'm becoming?

He reached out to new peers.
Joined a trauma group.
Learned to speak to himself with grace instead of shame.

Now? Isaiah is two years clean.
He speaks at rehabs and jails.
And he does it as someone who never gave up.

That's what becoming looks like:
- ⇒ Not a straight line.
- ⇒ But a sacred return.

Slip Debrief Card
A compassionate 5-minute check-in to turn any slip into learning.

1) What happened just before the slip? (people, place, feeling)
2) What did I tell myself in that moment?
3) What did I need that I didn't ask for?
4) What is one support I can add next time? (call, boundary, exit plan)
5) What is one sentence of grace I will say to myself now?

Close with:
**"I am still becoming.
This is information, not identity."**

Signal Check (3 quick questions)
- Where did this slip/urge/spiral point to a need (support, rest, boundary, skill)?
- What did I forget about who I'm becoming in that moment?
- What is one small repair I can make in the next 24 hours?
  (Reminder: A signal invites response. A sentence declares an ending. This is a signal.)

This Is the Shift

The old you thought:
"Once I fix myself, I'll be worthy."
"Once I have no cravings — then I'll matter."

The new you knows:
"I am worthy as I become."
"I don't have to earn my worth. I was born with it."
"I don't need to be perfect to be in progress."

This shift changes everything.
Because instead of striving to arrive, you start allowing yourself to evolve. You go from chasing a finished version to honoring the one unfolding.

From shame to self-compassion.
From punishment to patience.

Shame → Self-Compassion Translations
- ⇒ "I failed again." → "I had a setback; I can repair and keep going."
- ⇒ "I'm broken." → "I'm in a season of becoming."
- ⇒ "I should be further along." → "I'm moving at the pace that keeps me safe."
- ⇒ "I can't do this." → "I can't do this **yet**—and support helps."
- ⇒ "I ruined everything." → "I caused harm; I can own it and make amends."
- ⇒ "I'm behind." → "I'm on **my** path; comparison is just noise."
- ⇒ "I always mess up." → "I'm learning new skills; progress is uneven."
- ⇒ "No one can love me like this." → "I'm worthy of care while I heal."

Use these as training wheels for your inner voice; repeat the translation that fits each moment.

Three Signs You're Already Becoming

- Your language shifts: "I always mess up" becomes "I'm learning how to do this."
- Your pauses lengthen: you take one breath before you reply, decide, or react.
- Your environment reflects your values: fewer chaos cues, more calm cues (notes, routines, sleep, water, movement).

Circle the one you notice most this week and write a one-sentence example under it.

The truth is:
- Healing doesn't ask you to be flawless.
- It just asks you to stay present with yourself, one moment at a time.

Healing = Wholeness, Not Perfection

You don't need to have it all figured out to be worthy of love.
You don't need to have zero trauma to be making progress.
You don't heal by reaching a finish line.
You heal by accepting the process.

In nature, nothing is perfect — but everything belongs. Even the cracked tree, the wind-worn mountain, the broken shell on the shore. They are beautiful not despite the cracks, but because of them.

The Japanese art of **Kintsugi** repairs broken pottery with gold, not to hide the break — but to highlight it.

To say:
"This, too, is part of the story."

Your cracks don't disqualify you. They qualify you to walk with others who are healing, too.

Becoming Boundaries: say less, mean more
Use simple, clear sentences that match your new identity.

- "I don't do that anymore. I do this instead: _____."
- "I won't discuss this while voices are raised. I'm available at _____ to revisit it."
- "I am not available for self-criticism. Here's what I'm practicing instead: _____."
- "That doesn't work for me. What will work is: _____."
- "I'm choosing my peace here. I'm stepping away and will check back at _____."

Quick prompts:
1) Where am I over-explaining?
2) What is one boundary I can say in one sentence?

Rewriting the Identity Statement

Let's get honest. What story have you been telling yourself?

Step 1: Write the Old Story

"I'm broken."
"I ruin everything."
"I'm too damaged to recover."
"I'll never get it right."

Now breathe. That's the old tape.
Let's change it.

Step 2: Flip the Frame

"I'm in a season of becoming."
"My story is still unfolding."
"I've made it through 100% of my worst days. I'm still here."
"I'm learning. And that's enough."

Step 3: Say This Out Loud:
"I am not broken.
I am becoming.
And that's enough for today."

Say it in the mirror. Say it in the shower.
Say it before bed. Say it until it starts to feel real.
Your nervous system needs repetition.
Your soul needs gentleness.
This affirmation gives you both.

Evidence Log (7 days)
Each night, capture 3 proofs from the new script.
- "I paused before replying."
- "I asked for clarity instead of assuming."
- "I went to bed on time."

Template
Day ____ — Proofs I'm already becoming:

1. _____
2. _____

Small proofs stack into identity. Keep them where you can see them.

"Who Am I?" Journal Prompts
Try these questions this week in your notebook, mirror time, or group discussion:

⇒ Who am I becoming — when no one's watching?
⇒ What have I already survived that proves I'm stronger than I thought?
⇒ What's something the old me would've done — that the new me won't?

BELIEVE. BEHAVE. BECOME.

⇒ What's one soft thing I want to reclaim (laughter, rest, creativity, etc.)?
⇒ What would I say to my past self if I could speak love into their pain?
⇒ Where do I need more grace — not more grit?
⇒ What does becoming look like on a hard day?
⇒ What would the future me thank me for doing this week?

Write it.
Feel it.
Let it guide you forward.

Future You Voice Note
Record a 30-second message as the version of you you're becoming. Play it each morning and before bed.

Steps:
1. Open your phone's voice memos.
2. Speak in the present tense.
3. Keep it under 30 seconds.
4. Title it "Becoming – Daily."

Sample script
"I am not broken. I am becoming. Today I choose one calm breath, one honest boundary, one aligned action. I move with patience and self-respect. I'm proud of the way I return."

Becoming Journal Prompts
Theme: You Are Not Broken — You Are Becoming

So many people in recovery carry the lie that they're too far gone. This chapter is about dismantling that lie — and choosing a new lens:

- ◊ You are not broken.
- ◊ You are becoming.

STEP 1: RECOGNIZE THE OLD STORY
What did you used to believe about yourself that kept you feeling broken?

Examples:
"I ruin everything."
"I can't be trusted."
"I always mess it up."
"I'm not enough."
Write 2–3 of your old "identity statements" here:
_____
_____

Where do you think these came from? (Family? Society? Trauma?)
_____
_____

STEP 2: FLIP THE FRAME
Now rewrite each old belief into a "becoming" belief:
"I am not broken. I am becoming someone who _____."

"My story is still unfolding, and I am learning to _____."

"I've made it through 100% of my worst days. That makes me _____."

STEP 3: JOURNAL PROMPTS
Use one prompt per day or pick the ones that speak to you most.

1. Who am I becoming?
2. What have I already survived that proves I'm stronger than I thought?
3. What's something the old me would've done — that the new me won't?
4. What's one soft thing I want to reclaim (laughter, rest, creativity, etc.)? Why?
5. What would I say to my past self if I could speak love into their pain?

STEP 4: AFFIRM THE PROCESS
Say it aloud or write it again here to reinforce the shift:
"I am not broken.
I am becoming.
And that is enough for today."

Brain Science
Growth mindset isn't just motivational fluff — it's real science.

Studies by psychologist *Carol Dweck* show that using the word "yet" strengthens motivation and resilience.

Instead of:
"I can't do this."

Try:
"I can't do this... yet."

This small shift helps your brain rewire from shame to possibility.

The Gold Line Ritual
Write your loudest old identity sentence at the top of a page:

1) "I'm broken."
2) Draw one thin line across it (use any pen; think "gold" as a symbol of repair, not erasure).
3) Beneath the line, write your new sentence: "I am not broken. I am becoming."
4) Date it. Read it aloud once a day for seven days.
5) Keep the page where you'll see it (journal, wallet, nightstand).

This ritual does not erase your past. It reframes it. The line marks the moment you chose a different story—and began to live it.

30-Day Becoming Plan
Keep it simple. One identity, one action, one check-in.

Week 1
Identity focus: "I am a person who keeps small promises."
Daily action: one 2-minute behavior you can't miss.
Check-in: every night—Did I keep it? If not, why not?

Week 2
Identity focus: "I speak to myself with respect."
Daily action: rewrite harshness into a kinder sentence.
Check-in: note one moment your tone softened.

Week 3
Identity focus: "I choose regulated first responses."
Daily action: one physiological reset per day
Check-in: record one decision that went better.

Week 4
Identity focus: "I act like my future self in one place."
Daily action: pick one domain (sleep, money) and practice the future-you behavior daily.
Check-in: write three proofs each night that you showed up as that version.

Graduation line to write and read aloud:
"I am not broken. I am becoming. I can prove it to myself, one day at a time."

Personal Reflection

"My story is still being written. I'm still becoming."
That simple line carried me through one of the roughest nights of my recovery.

About three years in recovery, management at my sober living home claimed I'd failed a drug screen. I knew it wasn't true. My supervisor at work—also a close friend—had walked with me through a lot already. I told him what happened. He said he believed me. Policy didn't. I still had to pack my things.

That night I slept in one of the small trucks we used for our mobile laundry program. Anger. Shame. Fear of the unknown. All of it rushed in—until I reminded myself:
struggle grows me if I let it.

I kept repeating, *"My story is still being written. I'm still becoming."*

My wife stayed on FaceTime with me for hours. We were still dating at the time. I'll never forget how she loved on me that night. I really needed her love and in her own way she reminded me that I was still becoming, and it was only a moment that we'd look back on. It makes my heart happy to know she was correct.

I had to steer past my ego—the need to be right, the urge to clap back—and choose dignity.

Faithful in the meantime. Patient for the truth to surface. Anchored in that one line: ***"My story is still being written. I'm still becoming."*** It's a blessing to know that I stayed the course in becoming me.

Final Truth of This Chapter:

The caterpillar doesn't need to earn wings.
 It was always meant to fly.
 It doesn't hustle to prove it's worthy.
 It just becomes.

You don't have to prove yourself to become the person you were born to be. You just have to keep becoming —
with softness,
with truth,
with love.

Not *broken*.
 Becoming.
Not *behind*.
 Becoming.
Not *finished*.
 Becoming.

SECTION THREE

BECOME

Chapters 11-13

CHAPTER ELEVEN

You Are the Universe Remembering Itself

BELIEVE. BEHAVE. BECOME.

Let's zoom out for a second.
Really zoom out.
Not just from your circumstances.
Not just from your past.
But from the version the world tried to sell you.

You've read ten chapters about belief, emotion, healing, identity, behavior, and growth.

- ◊ You've peeled back layers.
- ◊ You've reclaimed pieces of yourself.
- ◊ You've started to live on purpose.

But here's the part nobody told you — the part the system, the shame, and the trauma tried to hide from you:

You are not just a person in recovery.
You are not just someone with a past.
You are not even just a human being.

You are the universe, in human form, waking up to your power.

You are life — aware of itself.
You are stardust with memory.

You are what happens when divine energy chooses to walk around in sneakers.

You step outside after a long day.
The city hums; your mind won't quit.
You glance up, feel small for a second—
then remember: those stars aren't just above you.
They're in you...

Stardust and Soul

Let's start with the science.
Astronomers and physicists have proven this:

- The calcium in your bones
- The iron in your blood
- The carbon in your cells
- The oxygen in your lungs

Science Snapshot: From Stars to You
- A star fuses light elements until it can't anymore.
- It collapses, then explodes—scattering heavier elements (iron, calcium, carbon) across space.
- Those atoms seed clouds → form new suns and planets → become oceans, soil, breath, bodies.
- Timeline: billions of years... right to your heartbeat.
- Translation: your blood's iron was forged in a star.

All of it came from stars that exploded billions of years ago.
When a star dies, it doesn't disappear.

It bursts.

And that explosion sends elements across galaxies —
And they made up your skin, your brain, your breath.

Literally — you are made of stardust.
That's not poetry.
That's physics.

And yet, it is poetic.
Something that sounds so cosmic is also your truth.
You don't just come from pain.
You come from power.

BELIEVE. BEHAVE. BECOME.

YouTube Break:
"You Are the Universe" – Neil deGrasse Tyson

In this clip, Dr. Tyson reminds us that we don't just live in the universe — we are the universe becoming conscious of itself.

He says:
"We are not figuratively, but literally stardust — and that makes us part of something ancient, beautiful, and powerful."

So What Does That Mean for Recovery?

It means:
You're not here just to survive.
You're not here just to stay out of jail or avoid relapse.
You're not here just to pay bills or get clean and call it done.

You're here to remember who you are.
- A creator.
- A builder.
- A being of light.
- A force of nature.
- A divine expression of energy, learning how to love itself again.

Everything you've walked through?
It didn't break you.
It prepared you.
It carved space inside you for something vast.

Because now that you know darkness — you can carry light.
You know what it's like to forget — so you can remember.
You've been humbled — so you can rise with purpose.

Recovery isn't just about healing old wounds.
It's about reclaiming your role in the big story.
The cosmic story.

Story in Action: Meet Elena

Elena grew up in the foster system.
She never knew where she came from — no baby pictures, no roots, no records of her birth parents.

In addiction, she felt small.
Like a mistake that somehow kept surviving.
She told herself, *"I'm just taking up space."*

But one night, during meditation at a women's trauma group, something shifted.

A thought floated up like a whisper:
*"You don't need a human family tree to know you belong.
You're part of something older."*

She cried.
Not because she was sad —
but because for the first time in her life, she felt connected.

Elena started looking at stars differently.
- She read about the Big Bang.
- She watched videos about black holes and galaxies.
- She started wearing a galaxy charm around her neck.

It reminded her:
"I come from that. I am that."

She didn't just believe in God anymore.
She believed she was made by God —
of God.

That changed everything.
Her posture. Her breath.
The way she forgave herself.
The way she showed up in the room.

She didn't need a last name to know who she was.
She was Elena, Child of the Cosmos.
A miracle in motion.

You Are Not Separate

One of the biggest lies trauma teaches is:
"You're alone."

And addiction adds:
- ⇒ "No one would understand anyway."
- ⇒ "Keep it all inside."
- ⇒ "Don't show weakness."

But healing teaches us:
"You're connected to everything."

You always were.

You're connected to:
- ◊ The sky that holds your breath
- ◊ The rivers that mirror your flow
- ◊ The trees that show you how to grow and let go
- ◊ The stars that remind you to shine
- ◊ The fire that warms
- ◊ The moon that cycles

- ◊ The seasons that turn
- ◊ The rhythm that beats in all things

You are not separate.
You are stitched into the fabric of everything.
Your heartbeat is part of a much bigger pulse.

And your healing matters — not just to you, but to all of us.
When you heal, you shift the frequency of the whole.
When you recall who you are, you help others recall.

Cosmic Identity Reconnection (Part 1)
Let's tap into your universal roots.

Step 1: Look Up
Tonight, find one star. Just one.
Even if it's cloudy, imagine it.
Let it be your anchor.
Breathe.

Let it be your reminder:
"I came from that."

If stars can explode, scatter, and become new life —
So can you.

Step 2: Repeat This Truth:
"I am the universe remembering itself through this body.
I am not a mistake.
I am a miracle in motion."

Say it until it no longer feels foreign.
Say it when you feel disconnected.
Say it when shame tries to creep in.

Step 3: Ask: What will I bring back to the world?
- Love?
- Peace?
- Laughter?
- Music?
- Healing?
- Hope?

You didn't come back from the edge just to exist.
You came back to illuminate.
This is how we become.

Visualization: Return to Wholeness

Close your eyes.
Sit with your breath.

Now picture your heart as a glowing star inside your chest.
A soft, pulsing light.
Each breath fans the flame.
It lights up your spine. Your mind. Your voice.
You begin to glow from within.

Now rise — in your imagination — above your old story.

See it like a landscape below you.
See how far you've come.
See the wounds, the wins, — all part of your becoming.

Now say softly to yourself:
*"I am not broken.
I am a return.
I am the light coming home."*

Let that settle in your bones.
Let it remind your cells:
You are home. In this body. In this universe. Right now.

YouTube Break:
1. "You Are Stardust – 963 Hz DNA Activation"
This frequency supports spiritual awakening. Use it during meditation, journaling, or silent reflection.

2. "Awakening Inner Light – 528 Hz + 963 Hz"
A harmonic blend to activate your cellular memory.
Let it wash over you as a reminder:
You were never lost. You were just remembering.

Cosmic Identity Reconnection (Part 2)
Theme: You Are the Universe Remembering Itself

You're not just someone in recovery.
You're not just a survivor of trauma.
You are literally made of stardust —
 and that means you're ancient, sacred, and powerful.

STEP 1: REMEMBER THE SCIENCE
Astronomers and physicists have proven:
- The calcium in your bones,
- The iron in your blood,
- The carbon in your cells —

All came from ancient stars that exploded billions of years ago.

Write this in your own words:
"What does it mean to you that you are literally made of stars?"

STEP 2: REMEMBER YOUR CONNECTION

Write one truth next to each force of nature below:

1. The Sky: How does it reflect your breath, freedom, or vastness?

2. The River: What does it teach you about emotions or flow?

3. The Trees: What do they show you about growth and letting go?

4. The Stars: What do they remind you of when you feel small or alone?

STEP 3: COSMIC AFFIRMATIONS

Complete these identity statements:
*"I am not just a person recovering.
I am the universe remembering how to _____."*

*"I am not broken.
I am made of _____ and I carry _____."*
*"My past does not define me.
My _____ does."*

STEP 4: VISUALIZATION – Return to Wholeness

You can do this with your eyes closed, or while journaling.

Imagine your heart as a glowing star.
Each breath fans its light.
See the light spreading up your spine... into your brain... through your hands and feet.

See yourself rising above your past like a phoenix.
Now say to yourself — or write here:
"I am not _____."
"I am a return to _____."
"I am the light coming home."

What does that image stir up in you?

STEP 5: PURPOSE REMEMBERING

What do you feel you are here to bring to the world?
(Love, wisdom, healing, laughter, peace, etc.)

Write it boldly:
"I am here to bring….."

Personal Reflection

I believe that when we learn to regulate this bioelectric system we call the body, we'll begin to access multi-dimensional experiences.

I've come to see that my body isn't just flesh and blood — it's a living antenna. A conduit of geometry, and intention.

The bioelectric fields flowing through me don't just influence my health — they shape how I perceive reality, what I believe is possible, and how deeply I can connect with something beyond the physical.

More and more, I sense that consciousness may not live in the brain at all — but in the silent, electric current that pulses between my cells and expands beyond them.

And when this system is finely tuned, something opens. My awareness stretches. Healing accelerates. Time bends. And things I once called miracles start to feel like mechanisms I'm finally beginning to understand.

Everything I place around or within me — water, crystals, copper, frequencies, light — becomes more than a ritual. They are modulators of my field. Tools that help me rewire access points I didn't know existed.

It's not fiction. It's electricity.
And somehow, in all of this, I realize I'm not just activating the body —
I'm awakening the cosmos inside it.
Because I am not just in the universe.

I am the universe — remembering itself — cell by cell, signal by signal, breath by breath."

Final Truth of This Chapter:

You are not your trauma.
- ⇒ You are not your past.
- ⇒ You are not your mistakes.
- ⇒ You are not the names they called you.
- ⇒ You are not the things you did in survival mode.

You are the universe waking up in a body.
- You are consciousness remembering itself.
- You are divine intelligence with a heartbeat.
- And now that you remember who you are — you're ready to become what you were born to be.

Bigger.
- Brighter.
- Bolder.
- Wiser.
- You.

You are not small.
You are not forgotten.
You are not separate from the divine.
You are the universe waking up through a human form.

**Let your recovery be a return,
not just to stability,
but to cosmic awareness.**

BELIEVE. BEHAVE. BECOME.

CHAPTER TWELVE

Walk Like It's Already Done

"When you shift from hoping to knowing, from wishing to walking — that's when you become it." — Unknown

Let's pause and look at how far you've come.

- You've done the hard work.
- You've faced your past.
- You've told the truth.
- You've built new beliefs.
- You've practiced new behaviors.
- You've reconnected with your inner self — and source.

And now there's only one thing left to do:
Walk like it's already done.

That doesn't mean ignore reality. It means start embodying your new truth — even before the proof shows up.

It means letting your actions reflect your identity before the world catches on, before they meet the real you...

This is where the *transformation* becomes **visible.**
This is where *belief* becomes behavior — in **motion.**

Don't Just Hope for the Future — Embody It

This is the chapter where you stop waiting to become the person you've been working on.

This is the moment where:
**You shift from intention to identity
From preparation to presentation
From "almost" to "already"**

You've already been planting seeds.
In your thoughts.
In your habits.
In your spirit.

Bridge Your Intention with a Plan
When **X** happens, I will **Y**.

◊ *When I feel the urge to isolate,* **I will text one safe person within 2 minutes.**
◊ *When I'm triggered in traffic,* **I will do two inhales/ long exhales before speaking.**
◊ *When shame shows up at bedtime,* **I will write one self-compassion line and set out tomorrow's first step.**

Pre-choosing the move turns identity into muscle memory.

Now it's time to walk like the harvest is coming.
Not just "someday." But now. This kind of walk doesn't mean pretending you have it all together.

It means **acting like your destiny is already in motion.**
You carry yourself like the future is unfolding — because it is.

Three Ways It Looks Today
Parent: Maya wanted to yell. Future-Maya knelt, breathed, and named the feeling. Bedtime ended in a hug, not a slam.
Student: Luis felt "behind." Future-Luis opened the laptop, set a 10-minute timer, and finished one paragraph.
Returning Citizen: Dre feared the interview. Future-Dre ironed his shirt, practiced his opener on the bus, and shook the manager's hand anyway.

Science Insight: Studies in neuroscience show that when you act "as if," your brain begins to rewire your identity.

According to *Dr. Joe Dispenza,* when your behaviors match your intention, your body starts to believe it's already experiencing the change — triggering new neural pathways. That's not just mindset. **That's biology.**

Recovery is a Walk

It's not about being "done."
It's about becoming daily.

And becoming daily requires:
1) Showing up when it's inconvenient
2) Making the call when you'd rather isolate
3) Speaking life when your old voice wants to judge
4) Saying yes to peace even when chaos is familiar
5) Holding your boundaries even when it feels lonely
6) Walking away when your ego wants to stay and fight

You become by walking in the truth until it becomes your new normal. **Because repetition creates reality.**

YouTube Break:
"Walk Like It's Already Yours – ET the Hip Hop Preacher"

In this powerful motivational video, Eric Thomas explains how high performers don't wait until they feel ready — they move like they already are.

He says:
***"Winners don't show up to get it.
They show up like they got it."***

When you walk like it's yours, the world starts responding to your energy differently.

Story in Action: Meet Xavier

Xavier came out of prison with two outfits, no job, and a vision of opening a nonprofit for teens.

Everyone said, "Start small."
But Xavier?
He walked like it was already done.

He carried a notebook with his mission written down.

- He studied grant writing on YouTube.
- He practiced his elevator pitch on the bus.
- He showed up to community events in a clean button-up and tie — even when others came in hoodies.

Did he have the office yet? **No.**
The grant funding? **Not yet.**
But his walk was different.
His energy was different.

He didn't wait for permission. He gave himself the authority. One year later — his program got picked up by the city.
Not because he waited…
But because he walked like it was already his.

Recovery Reflection: When people asked Xavier how he got so far, he said: *"I had to act like I was worth it before* *anyone else believed it. That's what kept me going when I had nothing but vision."*

This Isn't Pretending. This Is Alignment.

There's a difference between pretending and embodying.

Pretending is rooted in fear — trying to be someone you're not. **Alignment** is rooted in truth — stepping into who you already are, as you become.

When what you **believe, say, do**, and **how you carry yourself** point the same direction, you become unstoppable.

Your **reticular activating system (RAS)** filters what you notice. When you walk like it's already done, your brain starts seeking and recognizing opportunities that match that identity. **Embodiment creates momentum.**

60-Second RAS Spotlight Drill
Your brain notices what you tell it matters. Aim the spotlight.

- ◊ **Morning (10s):** Read your identity line once: "I am a _____."
- ◊ **Midday (30s):** List 3 tiny signals that matched it today (e.g., calm reply, boundary kept, water instead of soda).
- ◊ **Evening (20s):** Circle one and write one sentence: "This is evidence I'm becoming."

Tip: Set 2 phone reminders named "Spotlight: AM / PM" for the next 7 days.

BELIEVE. BEHAVE. BECOME.

Even if the world hasn't caught on yet — your nervous system does. Your spirit knows. And the universe begins to mirror your inner alignment. That's why **embodiment creates momentum.**

New Walk, Old Audience
Not everyone will recognize your change right away. Some knew your old patterns. That's okay—keep walking.

If they tease your growth:
"I'm practicing a different response now. I'd love your support."

If they doubt your motive:
"I get why it feels new. I'm still learning. Today I'm choosing this because it aligns with who I'm becoming."

If they try to pull you back:
"I'm serious about this. If you can't respect it, I'm going to take some space."

Reminder: *Their memory isn't your destiny. Stay aligned.*

Personal Reflection

I still believe in "make-believe."
Truthfully, I think we're all still playing it. Some of us are aware — and intentionally make what we believe.
Most do not.

It takes a trained imagination to curate a taste for the future **now**.

For me, my past identity was made up of old programs and traumatic memories. Recovery became my chance to rewrite that story — to become the version of myself I'd always glimpsed but never fully lived. And that version could be anyone I chose to become.

Once I had a clear image of that new version — someone passionate about helping others in recovery — I had to do more than just imagine him. I had to *become* him. I had to take what I believed about myself and make it real.

I didn't want a mirage. I wanted something lasting. Tangible. So I committed to the process — learning, unlearning, practicing. I had to understand how real change actually happens, and choose to practice my lessons in real life.

In private, I would act out scenes from the life I was building — like an actor preparing for a role. I'd talk through conversations from my future, rehearse my lines, and explore the emotions behind my character's growth.

That was my method. And it turns out, I'm not alone. Many of my favorite people have done the same — predicting who they'd become before the world caught up. Something shifted when those imagined scenes became real in my life.

I can't speak for anyone else, but I know this: by making a habit of living out my visualizations, I shortened the distance between thought and manifestation.

Practice: Walk It Like It's Already Done

Step 1 — Name the identity you're walking in.

- "I am a healed woman who leads others."
- "I am a father who shows up daily."
- "I am a man of peace, not chaos."

BELIEVE. BEHAVE. BECOME.

- "I am a leader in recovery."
- "I am a creative force, not a victim of circumstance."
- "I am the healed version of me—walking in real time."

Step 2 — Ask: *How would this version of me move through today?*

- What would they wear/eat/listen to?
- How would they respond to stress?
- What would they post—or not post?
- Would they waste time…or pour into purpose?

Step 3 — Walk in it. Now.
Even if you're scared. Even if nobody claps. Even if results aren't here yet. **You walk first; results follow.**

Impostor Flare Plan

New ≠ fake. New = unfamiliar.
When that **"who do you think you are?"** voice pops up:

1) Name it: "This is an impostor flare, not a fact."
2) Narrow the moment: "What's the next 60-second aligned action?"
3) Normalize the wobble: "Shaky is still steady if it's in the right direction."

Close with one breath and one step. Proof beats panic.

If–Then Obstacle Planner

Walking like it's already done doesn't mean you won't hit friction. It means you plan for it.

Trigger → Old Autopilot → New If–Then

• If I wake up anxious, then I will do 2 slow "physiological sighs" and read my identity line out loud.

• If a last-minute request hits my phone, then I will pause 10 seconds, check my calendar, and reply honestly: "I can't this time."

• If I'm running late and want to skip group, then I will text a peer "Joining 10 mins late—hold me a seat."

• If criticism stings, then I will shoulders-back + long exhale and say, "Thanks for the input—I'll consider it," instead of defending.

• If an urge to numb shows up, then I will set a 5-minute timer, drink water, and message my support person before deciding anything.

Your turn (add 3):

1) If _____ then I will _____.

2) If _____ then I will _____.

3) If _____ then I will _____.

Bonus Tool: Morning Identity Walk
Before your feet hit the floor, say aloud:

BELIEVE. BEHAVE. BECOME.

- "Today I walk like the person I'm becoming."
- "My energy matches my destiny."
- "I show up in full alignment."
- "I do not shrink. I embody. I expand."

Then stand. Three slow breaths. Tall posture. Shoulders soft. Chin lifted. **Feel the version of you that's already home in your body.**

Tip: If possible, do a brief barefoot walk outside (earthing). Grounding is linked with reduced inflammation, better sleep, and steadier emotions.

Embodiment Micro-Habits (1–3 minutes)
Pick one per time slot. Consistency > intensity.

- **Before work:** 4-7-8 breath x2 • Stand tall, chin level, name your value for the day
- **In transit:** Walk 40 steps "like it's already done" • Whisper your identity line on each exhale
- **At meals:** 3 conscious breaths before first bite • "I nourish the future me"
- **After conflict:** Hand on chest + long exhale • "I choose repair over reactivity"
- **Social scroll:** Pause, place phone down, take 3 steps and ask, "What would future-me do next?"
- **Evening reset:** Two-sentence gratitude + one "evidence" line from today
- **Accountability ping:** Text a trusted person, "Today I walked like _____. Win: _____."

Pick 2 to repeat daily for a week. Let them become your body's default.

7-Day Embodiment Challenge

A week of tiny, repeatable reps that teach your body who you are now, not who you used to be.

How it works:
- Each morning, read your identity line once: "I am a _____."
- Do the day's one action.
- That night, write one evidence sentence: "Proof I'm becoming: _____."

Day 1 — Posture rep: Stand tall for 60 seconds before your first conversation.
Day 2 — Boundary rep: Say one honest no or one clear yes you mean.
Day 3 — Breath rep: Two physiological sighs before you reply to any stress.
Day 4 — Language rep: Swap one self-put-down for your identity line.
Day 5 — Repair rep: If you get sharp, circle back and repair in one sentence.
Day 6 — Focus rep: Ten uninterrupted minutes on one meaningful task.
Day 7 — Environment rep: Lay out tomorrow's clothes and a two-line agenda.

End-of-week prompt: What felt easiest? What created the biggest shift?

Walk Audit (2 minutes)
Midday, check the signals your body is sending.
Circle one word for each, or jot a quick note.
- Posture: collapsed / neutral / open
- Pace: rushed / steady / intentional
- Breath: shallow / mixed / deep

- Tone: sharp / flat / warm
- Eye contact: avoiding / inconsistent / present
- Choice quality: reactive / mixed / aligned

Now pick one micro-tweak for the next hour:
"I will slow my pace by 10% and breathe before I speak."
"I will finish one task before switching."
"I will replace one complaint with one solution sentence."

Evening note: One line of evidence you walked in alignment today.

Soundtrack for Stepping Into It
- *"I AM Walking Into My Destiny"* – Affirmations Loop
- *"Step Like a Leader"* – Daily Affirmations Over 432Hz

This affirmation loop uses heart-centered frequency to align mind, breath, and identity.

Walk Like It's Already Done

Recovery isn't waiting until you "arrive." It's **walking in your truth**—daily, boldly, imperfectly—like the version of you that already exists. This worksheet helps you move from **hoping → knowing → embodying**.

Step 1 — Claim the Identity
Write the identity you're stepping into:
"I am a _____."

Examples

- "I am a healed woman who leads others."
- "I am a father who shows up daily."
- "I am a man of peace, not chaos."
- "I am a leader in recovery."

Your turn:
"I am a

_____
_____."

Step 2 — Embody the Energy
How would that version of you move through today?

- What would they wear?
- How would they answer the phone?
- What messages would they send?
- How would they carry themselves?
- What would they post (or not)?
- Which thoughts would they entertain—and which would they reject?

Step 3 — Walk in It
This isn't faking; it's aligning. When beliefs, words, actions, and energy point the same way, you shift from **becoming → being**.

Circle one for today: Aligned / Confident / Present / Worthy / Focused / Unshakable / Other: _____
One small action to walk in alignment today:

_____

Bonus Tool — Morning Identity Walk

Before your feet hit the floor, say:

- "Today I walk like the person I'm becoming."
- "My energy matches my destiny."
- "I show up in full alignment."

BELIEVE. BEHAVE. BECOME.

Your custom morning mantra:
_____
_____

You don't have to wait to be ready.
You don't have to wait for applause.
You don't have to wait for results.

You walk first and the results follow your energy.
Walk like the healing is happening.
Walk like your future is already unfolding.
Walk like the proof is in your posture.

Environment Upgrade Checklist

Make your surroundings quietly confirm who you are now.

Phone: Lock screen = your one-line identity. Remove one distracting app.
Closet: Lay out tomorrow's outfit that matches how you want to feel (calm, ready, clean).
Desk/Backpack: Keep one anchor object (coin, bracelet, note) you touch before hard tasks.
Car/Commute: Queue a 3–5 minute affirmation loop or breath track.
Kitchen: Place your water bottle where you'll see it; speak an intention before first sip.
Doorway: Tape a tiny card at eye level: "Enter as the future you."

Small upgrades, big alignment.

Weekly Becoming Review (10 minutes)

1) One moment I walked in alignment:

_____
_____.

2) One moment I drifted—and how I "walked it back":
_____
_____.

3) One boundary I honored (or will repair this week):
_____
_____.

4) One relationship that felt better because I showed up different:
_____
_____.

5) Carry-forward: One micro-action I'll repeat daily next week: "I will
_____
_____."

Close with: "I walk first. Results follow."

Final Truth of This Chapter

You don't become powerful **after** people believe in you. You become powerful the day **you** believe — and start walking like it.

Walk like the peace is already yours.
Walk like the family restoration is happening.
Walk like the opportunity already has your name on it.
Walk like the miracle already occurred.

BELIEVE. BEHAVE. BECOME.

Because in a way — it already has.
You're still here.
And that is no small thing.
The person you've become through these chapters?
They've always been in you.

Now, One Last Word Before We Go...
You've made it through **Believe.**
You've practiced how to **Behave.**
And now... you are starting to **Become.**

But before we close this book, there's one more truth.
One more healing message that ties it all together.

CHAPTER THIRTEEN

You Were the Blueprint All Along

BELIEVE. BEHAVE. BECOME.

"You're not chasing the dream.
You are the dream — remembering itself."
— Anonymous

You thought this was a recovery book.
 But really?
This is a resurrection manual.

You thought you were trying to fix yourself.
 But the truth is — you were trying to return to yourself.
 Not to the version that got hurt.
 But to the version that always existed beneath the pain.

You were never the problem.

You were the portal — the doorway back to power.
And all this time, you've been waiting on something…

- ◊ A sign.
- ◊ A shift.
- ◊ A Savior.

But now you know:

- You were the sign.
- You were the shift.
- You were the Savior.
- You didn't need to be rescued.
- You needed to wake up and RISE!

And now that you've remembered?
You're becoming unstoppable.

The Holy Grail Was Never Hidden

Let's shatter the myth.

There's no secret code.

- ⇒ No outside permission.
- ⇒ No gatekeeper.
- ⇒ No golden scroll tucked away in some mountain.
- ⇒ No white-robed master holding the key to your worth.

The Grail is you:
- Waking up.
- Taking responsibility.
- Reclaiming your power.
- Refusing to abandon yourself.
- Learning to be with your own fire.
- Realizing you're both the storm and the stillness.

There was never a lock – only your permission.
There was never a delay – only your agreement.

You were never meant to beg life to love you.
You were meant to become life — and love yourself.

Spiritual Science Insight:

The Gospel of Thomas — one of the ancient texts hidden for centuries — says: *"If you bring forth what is within you, what you bring forth will save you."*

That's not just scripture – that's source code.
The Grail is within. Always was. Always will be.

BELIEVE. BEHAVE. BECOME.
The Grail = Creator Consciousness

Every step has brought you closer to remembering:
- You are not just a survivor of your past.
- You are a creator of what comes next.
- You weren't just learning to cope.
- You were learning to co-create.

And the moment you shift from reacting to creating — everything changes…

You stop chasing healing. You **become** it.
You stop needing proof. You **embody** the truth.
You stop waiting for signs. You **are** the signal.

Real-Life Shift

Alicia, a peer support leader in recovery, used to say:
"If I don't see it, I build it. That's what recovery taught me. I don't have to wait for permission to create what I need."

That's the Grail mindset.
That's what **becoming** is all about.

YouTube Break:
"The Creator Self" – Gregg Braden

In this clip, Braden explains how heart-brain coherence allows you to influence matter with emotion and belief. It's not magic. It's quantum alignment.

Another Program, or Permission?
Yes — programs help.
Yes — tools matter.

But at some point... you'll stop looking for another system and start trusting your soul.

Let this chapter be your permission slip:
1. To walk in power — even if nobody claps.
2. To speak like the healed version of you — even if your voice shakes.
3. To build like your future is guaranteed — even if no one else believes it yet.
4. To rest like the war is over — even if your nervous system is still learning.
5. To move like destiny is already catching up to your energy — because it is.

This is not hype.
This is reality-shifting recognition.

Because the person you've been becoming this whole time? They've always been in you.

Neuroscience Note:
According to *Dr. Caroline Leaf*, identity is formed through repetition and internalization.

When you give yourself permission to walk like it's done, your brain literally rewires your neural networks to support that identity. You're not faking it. You're forming it.

YouTube Break:
"This Is the Great Remembering – Alan Watts Compilation"

Alan Watts says:
*"You are not a drop in the ocean.
You are the entire ocean, in a drop."*

This is what Become really means.
Not "becoming someone new."
But becoming who you always were — before the world told you otherwise.

Before the labels.
Before the shame.
Before the diagnoses.
Before the silence.

Your true self didn't disappear.
It just got covered.

This chapter peels it back.
And hands you the mirror.

Personal Reflection

This journey I'm on is a journey of self-love. In 2025 it's hard for a lot of us to focus—especially those of us in recovery. Noise, desire, fear, automation, and numbness pull our attention outward and dim the signal of the light within.

If I had telepathy, I'd beam you the love I feel inside. Since I can't, this book is my transmission—my process for tapping lasting change, structured as a blueprint you can follow toward your own self-revelation.

I'm also learning it isn't only the recovery community that's mid-transformation. We all are. We all want a life rooted in self-love so we can love each other better. We all want resonance on this planet—but resonance begins inside.

And yes, it takes work:
- ◊ Unlearning the old programs.
- ◊ Writing new ones in our own voice.
- ◊ Moving our energy from shame, guilt, and fear toward love, compassion, and empathy.
- ◊ Rehearsing the future now—in ordinary moments—until it feels familiar.
- ◊ Recording affirmations and looping them until they become our subconscious default.
- ◊ Using imagination as the cosmic operating system it truly is.
- ◊ Showing up consistently until the outer world reorganizes around our inner alignment.

Simple, not easy. But this is the work that returns you to yourself—until the future you've been practicing meets you where you stand. I'm only one of many helpers along the way, like the many who have helped me...

The Creator Mirror Affirmations

Tonight, go to your mirror.
Look into your eyes — past the shame, the noise, the past.

Take a breath.
Another.
Feel your feet on the ground.
Place your hand over your chest.

And say:
"I remember who I am.
I create what I speak.
I move what I believe.
I align with what I deserve.
I am the blueprint.

BELIEVE. BEHAVE. BECOME.

*I am the Grail.
I am the proof."*

Say it again. Slowly. Until something unlocks.
Then smile. Because you made it.

Not just through this book.
- ⇒ But through death and rebirth.
- ⇒ Through forgetting and remembering.
- ⇒ Through fear... and into fire.
- ⇒ Through trauma... and into truth.
- ⇒ Through isolation... and into integration.

Journal Prompt:

- What parts of me am I reclaiming now that I remember I'm the Grail?
- What does my life look like when I stop waiting for signs — and start being the sign?
- Who would I be if I believed it was already mine?

YouTube Break:
"*You Are the Answer – 963 Hz Awakening Music*"

Let this play while you look in the mirror or write your truth.
Let your nervous system feel what it's like to be home again.

The Creator Mirror Exercise
Theme: I Am the Blueprint. I Am the Grail.

PART 1: LOOK IN THE MIRROR
This practice is not about how you look.
It's about how you see.

Tonight, or first thing in the morning, stand in front of a mirror. Look into your eyes.

Breathe. And ask yourself:
"Who have I been trying to become — that I already am?"
Write what comes up:
_____

PART 2: I AM NOT... / I AM...
Let's rewrite the old lies.
Write 3 lies the world or your past tried to convince you of:
"I am _____."
"I'll never _____."
"I'm not worthy of _____."

Now flip the script.
Write the truth your Creator Self knows:
"I am _____."
"I am becoming _____."
"I am worthy of _____."

PART 3: SHIFT INTO CREATOR CONSCIOUSNESS
The Creator doesn't wait for permission — the Creator creates.

Journal Prompt:
What area of your life are you waiting on something outside of you to change...when the change could start with you?

Write it out:

_____
_____.

What's one inspired action I can take today to create momentum?

Write it out:

_____
_____.

PART 4: DAILY ACTIVATION SCRIPT
Use this as a daily mirror ritual, or record it in your voice and listen during meditation:

*"I remember who I am.
I create what I speak.
I move what I believe.
I align with what I deserve.
I am the blueprint.
I am the Grail.
I am the proof."*

How did it feel to say those words?
_____
_____.

What resistance or emotion came up?
_____
_____.

What truth landed the deepest?

CREATOR VISION MAP
Describe your "creator era."

Not who you were, or even who you're trying to fix — but the force you are now stepping into.

Use this prompt to begin:
*"In my creator era,
I_____.*

YouTube Break:
"The Blueprint is You – 963 Hz DNA Upgrade + Self-Realization"

Let this play while doing your mirror work, journaling, or vision mapping. Let your cells remember.

Closing Transmission

This is not the end. This is the beginning.
Of your creator era. Of your designed reality.
Of your sovereign return.

Walk in it.
Own it.
Live it.

Science Spark: Intention trains what you notice (RAS). What you notice shapes what you do.

BELIEVE. BEHAVE. BECOME.
What you do rewires who you are.

Loop: *Intention → Attention → Action → Identity.*

Your first 72 hours
Today (15 min): Pick one identity line and record it in your voice. Play it while you walk.
Tomorrow (10 min): One aligned act you've avoided (text, call, form, boundary). Do it.
Day 3 (10 min): Write three "tiny proofs" you created this week—no matter how small.

If I wobble:
Pause (two breaths).
Name it: "A wave, not a verdict."
Reach out: text ____ / call ____ / group ____.
Repair one thing within 24 hours.
Repeat your line: "I am the return."

The Creator's Oath
I will not abandon myself.
I will walk in what I know, not wait for permission.
I will speak life over my body, my day, my name.
I will make my next move my proof.
I will return—again and again—until return is my rhythm.

Because the real "Holy Grail"…
was the version of you that never gave up.
The one that kept reading.
The one that kept breathing.
The one that kept becoming — even when it was hard.

Even when nobody saw. Even when you didn't feel ready.
And now?

You're ready to become everything you came here to be.
No longer chasing the dream.

Because you are the dream — remembering itself.

As above, so below:
as within, so without.

BELIEVE. BEHAVE. BECOME.

Resources

YouTube Breaks

1) **528 Hz Frequency — The Love Vibration**
2) **Acting Like the Person You Want to Be —** Mel Robbins
3) **Awakening Inner Light — 528 Hz + 963 Hz**
4) **Biology of Belief, The —** Dr. Bruce Lipton
5) **Breaking Generational Trauma —** Dr. Thema Bryant
6) **Change Your Story, Change Your Life —** Tony Robbins
7) **Creator Self, The —** Gregg Braden
8) **Emotional Release & Soothing Frequencies — 432Hz + 528Hz**
9) **Fake It Till You Make It? —** Dr. Andrew Huberman
10) **How to Feel Your Feelings —** Gabor Maté
11) **How to Rewire Your Brain —** Dr. Andrew Huberman
12) **I AM Affirmations — 432 Hz Manifestation Loop**
13) **Lies We Inherit, The —** Oprah & Dr. Shefali
14) **Power of Movement, The —** Steven Furtick
15) **Power of Neuroplasticity, The —** Dr. Joe Dispenza
16) **Power of Play, The —** Brené Brown
17) **Power of Yet, The (Growth Mindset) —** Carol Dweck
18) **Self-Love Affirmations | 528 Hz Healing Frequency**
19) **This Is the Great Remembering (Compilation) —** Alan Watts
20) **Walk Like It's Already Yours —** Eric Thomas (ET)
21) **You ARE Energy —** Dr. Joe Dispenza
22) **You Are Stardust — 963 Hz DNA Activation**
23) **You Are the Answer — 963 Hz Awakening Music**

24) **You Are the Universe** — Neil deGrasse Tyson
25) **Your Brain Predicts Reality** — Lisa Feldman Barrett

BELIEVE. BEHAVE. BECOME.

Resources

Public Figures

1. ***Abraham-Hicks (Esther Hicks)*** — Law of Attraction teachings.
2. ***Dr. Lisa Feldman Barrett*** — predictive brain & constructed emotion.
3. ***Boogie Down Productions (KRS-One)*** — early conscious hip-hop.
4. ***Gregg Braden*** — heart–brain coherence; science–spirit bridge.
5. ***Brené Brown*** — shame, courage, vulnerability research.
6. ***Dr. Thema Bryant*** — trauma psychologist & minister; generational healing.
7. ***Dr. Joe Dispenza*** — neuroplasticity + meditation for change.
8. ***Carol Dweck*** — growth mindset ("yet").
9. ***Masaru Emoto*** — water-crystal imagery & intention experiments.
10. ***Steven Furtick*** — pastor; action/faith messages.
11. ***Robert J. Gilbert*** — teacher of sacred geometry/energy studies.
12. ***Grandmaster Flash & the Furious Five*** — pioneering hip-hop ("The Message").
13. ***Dr. David R. Hawkins*** — "Map of Consciousness" emotional scale.
14. ***Louise Hay*** — mirror work; self-healing affirmations.
15. ***Dr. Andrew Huberman*** — neuroscience-based behavior protocols.
16. ***Ice-T*** — rapper/actor; street social narrative.
17. ***Dr. Martin Luther King Jr.*** — civil-rights leader; faith in action.

18. ***Dr. Caroline Leaf*** — cognitive neuroscientist; mind management.
19. ***Dr. Bruce Lipton*** — cell biologist; beliefs/environment and biology.
20. ***Gabor Maté, MD*** — addiction & trauma: "not why the addiction—why the pain."
21. ***N.W.A.*** — influential West Coast rap; social commentary.
22. ***Tony Robbins*** — motivational strategist; identity & state change.
23. ***Dr. Shefali Tsabary*** — conscious parenting & deconditioning.
24. ***Eric Thomas (ET)*** — motivational speaker; relentless execution.
25. ***Neil deGrasse Tyson*** — astrophysicist; "we are stardust."
26. ***Dr. Bessel van der Kolk*** — *The Body Keeps the Score*; trauma in the body.
27. ***Alan Watts*** — philosopher; non-duality & presence.
28. ***Oprah Winfrey*** — media leader; personal growth convos.

BELIEVE. BEHAVE. BECOME.

ABOUT THE AUTHOR

Jeff Vickers is a recovery coach (CCAR-trained RCP), author of *Sober Slogans*. He builds practical, hope-driven systems for newcomers in recovery and returning citizens—blending CBT/DBT-style tools with visualization, breathwork, and guided meditations.

After thirty years of active use, including sixteen years incarcerated, Jeff rebuilt his life in recovery and now helps others do the same. He is completing Alabama's CRSS pathway through the Department of Mental Health, and he's an active NAMI member. Through one-on-one coaching and group work, Jeff focuses on simple daily practices, accountability, and mindset skills people can use right away.

Jeff keeps a small client load year-round and speaks with community partners, churches, and reentry programs about building peer-led recovery ecosystems. Learn more and find his blogs and ebooks at **www.iamjeffvickers.com**. For serious inquiries: **iamjeffvickers@gmail.com**.

JEFF VICKERS

www.ingramcontent.com/pod-product-compliance
Lightning Source LLC
Chambersburg PA
CBHW060354080526
44583CB00012B/310